Cusco Peru Travel Guide 2023 - 2024

Discover the Wonders of Ancient History, Indulge in Local Cuisine, Unearth the Finest Accommodations, and Embark on Memorable Adventures.

Alex Fowler

Table of Contents

Chapter 1: Introduction
  Best Time to Visit
Chapter 2: Getting to Cusco
  By Air
  By Train
  By Bus
Chapter 3: Exploring Cusco City
  Plaza de Armas
  Cusco Cathedral
  Sacsayhuaman
  Qorikancha (Temple of the Sun)
  San Pedro Market
  Museums and Art Galleries
Chapter 4: Sacred Valley of the Incas
  Pisac
  Ollantaytambo
  Moray
  Maras Salt Mines
Chapter 5: Machu Picchu
  Planning Your Visit
  How to Get to Machu Picchu
  Guided Tours vs. Independent Visits
  Hiking the Inca Trail
Chapter 6: Surrounding Archaeological Sites
  Choquequirao
  Tipon

Piquillacta
Chapter 7: Cultural Experiences
Traditional Festivals
Peruvian Cuisine
Local Arts and Crafts
Chapter 8: Outdoor Activities
Hiking and Trekking
Rafting and Kayaking
Mountain Biking
Chapter 9: Practical Information
Accommodation Options
Local Transportation
Safety Tips
Language and Communication
Chapter 10: Cusco's Surroundings
Rainbow Mountain
Ausangate Trek
Manu National Park
Chapter 11: Sustainable Travel in Cusco
Responsible Tourism Practices
Community-Based Tourism Initiatives
Chapter 12: Traveling with Kids in Cusco
Family-Friendly Activities
Tips for Parents
Chapter 13: Useful Phrases and Vocabulary
Chapter 14: Resources
Recommended Reading
Helpful Websites and Apps
Maps and Navigation

Chapter 15: Conclusion

Chapter 1: Introduction

Peru, a region of magnificent scenery, historical civilizations, and lively culture, is a mesmerising destination for travellers from across the globe. This South American jewel provides a range of activities, from touring the famed ruins of Machu Picchu to immersing oneself in the rich customs of its indigenous villages. In this complete introduction to Peru for travellers, we will dig into its history, geography, sights, food, and more, to offer you with a broad knowledge of this wonderful nation.

1. Geography and Climate

Peru's geographical variety is extraordinary, spanning from the barren coastal plains to the towering Andes Mountains and the lush Amazon rainforest. The nation is separated into three different regions: the coastal area to the west, the Andean mountains in the middle, and the Amazon rainforest to the east. This geographical variance gives birth to an assortment of microclimates, making Peru a year-round destination for those seeking varied experiences.

2. History and Civilization

Peru possesses an ancient history that precedes the Inca civilisation. The area was home to various pre-Columbian civilizations, including the Moche, Nazca, and Chimu, each leaving behind interesting archaeological sites. However, it was the Inca Empire that governed over Peru from the 15th century until the Spanish invasion in the 16th century. Their remarkable construction and engineering may still be seen today at prominent places like Machu Picchu, Cusco, and the Sacred Valley.

3. Machu Picchu and the Inca Trail

Machu Picchu, the "Lost City of the Incas," is one of the most renowned archaeological sites in the world. Perched high in the Andes Mountains, this historic castle shows the genius of Inca architecture and provides breathtaking panoramic vistas. The Inca Trail, a famous hiking trail, enables brave tourists to follow in the footsteps of the Incas and culminates in a spectacular dawn vista of Machu Picchu.

4. Cusco and the Sacred Valley

The city of Cusco, originally the capital of the Inca Empire, is a dynamic and culturally rich destination. Its colonial architecture combines harmoniously with Inca masonry, providing a distinct ambience. The adjacent Sacred Valley is studded with historic monuments, traditional marketplaces, and gorgeous communities, offering insight into the Andean way of life.

5. Lake Titicaca

Straddling the border between Peru and Bolivia, Lake Titicaca is the world's highest navigable lake. Its crystal-clear waters are home to various indigenous groups living on man-made floating islands, showing their distinct cultures and traditions.

6. The Amazon Rainforest

For wildlife aficionados, a visit to the Peruvian Amazon is a must. The deep forest teems with wildlife, from colorful birds to secretive jaguars. Guided tours and eco-lodges give an opportunity to explore this biodiverse wonderland responsibly and develop a greater knowledge of the necessity of conservation.

7. Colca Canyon

Located in southern Peru, Colca Canyon is one of the deepest canyons in the world, exceeding even the Grand Canyon. The area is famed for its stunning scenery, quaint communities, and the possibility to view Andean condors flying over the sky.

8. Peruvian Cuisine

Peruvian cuisine has received worldwide praise for its combination of tastes, merging indigenous ingredients with influences from Spanish, African, and Asian civilizations. Ceviche, a meal of fresh fish marinated in citrus liquids, is a national favorite, while other highlights include lomo saltado, anticuchos, and a variety of potato-based dishes.

9. Festivals and Traditions

Peruvians take tremendous delight in maintaining their old customs and appreciating their unique cultural heritage. Throughout the year, several colorful festivals take place, with brilliant parades, traditional dances, and ornate costumes. Inti Raymi, the Festival of the Sun, celebrated in Cusco around the winter solstice, is one of the most major events.

10. Modern Peru

While Peru's historical heritage is alluring, the nation has also embraced modernity. The capital city, Lima, is a busy metropolis with a booming culinary scene, world-class museums, and dynamic neighborhoods. Other cities like Arequipa and Trujillo merge history with contemporary conveniences, creating a distinct urban experience.

Best Time to Visit

Choosing the ideal time to visit Peru may drastically affect your travel experience, since the country's unique topography and temperature provide various sights and activities throughout the year. From the towering Andes Mountains to the lush Amazon rainforest and the parched coastal plains, Peru's varied regions each have their own distinct weather patterns and seasonal highlights. In this detailed guide, we will investigate the ideal time to visit Peru for visitors, taking into consideration the weather, festivals, activities, and more.

1. Coastal Region (Lima, Paracas, Nazca):

The coastline area of Peru suffers a desert environment, with scorching temperatures and relatively little rainfall. The greatest time to visit this location is during the austral summer, which stretches from December to March. The weather is beautiful and suitable for touring the capital city, Lima, and its neighbouring attractions. However, be prepared for excessive humidity and the occasional coastal fog known as "garúa."

2. Andean Highlands (Cusco, Machu Picchu, Sacred Valley):

The Andean highlands have two different seasons: the dry season and the rainy season. The dry season extends from May to September, making it the perfect time to explore this area. During these months, you may enjoy bright sky and low rainfall, offering good conditions for walking the Inca Trail and visiting Machu Picchu.

3. Rainforest Region (Iquitos, Puerto Maldonado, Manu National Park):

The Amazon jungle endures a tropical environment with high humidity and significant rains year-round. However, there are two primary seasons: the rainy season and the dry season. The dry season, from May to October, is considered the greatest time to explore the rainforest, since there are less mosquitos and greater prospects for animal watching.

4. Lake Titicaca (Puno, Uros Floating Islands):

Lake Titicaca, situated in the Andean highlands, has a similar climate to Cusco and the surrounding regions. The dry season, from May to September, provides the most favourable weather for visiting the lake and its distinctive floating islands.

5. Northern Coast (Trujillo, Chiclayo, Mancora):

The northern coast of Peru enjoys a desert environment with warm temperatures throughout the year. However, it is crucial to remember that this area has its unique microclimates owing to the effect of the frigid Humboldt Current. The greatest time to visit the northern shore is during the austral summer, from December to March when the weather is bright and mild.

Festivals and Events:

Peru is a nation steeped in cultural traditions, and visiting during festivals may offer a distinct and lively depth to your vacation. Here are some prominent festivals and events in Peru:

- Inti Raymi: Celebrated on June 24th in Cusco, Inti Raymi is the Festival of the Sun, an ancient Inca ceremonial celebration to celebrate the sun deity. It is one of the most prominent and colorful festivities in Peru.

- Carnaval: This boisterous event takes place in February or March, depending on the date of Easter. Different areas of Peru have their own distinct methods of celebrating Carnaval, including water battles, music, dancing, and traditional costumes.

- Semana Santa (Holy Week): Occurring in the week preceding up to Easter, Semana Santa is honoured across the nation with processions, religious rites, and spectacular street decorations.

- Fiesta de la Candelaria: Celebrated in Puno during the first two weeks of February, this event mixes Andean customs with Catholicism and incorporates spectacular parades and traditional dances.

Activities and Highlights by Season:

- Dry Season (May to September): - Trekking the Inca Trail to Machu Picchu and other Andean routes.

- Exploring the Sacred Valley and its archaeological sites.

- Visiting the Amazon jungle for animal watching.

- Enjoying water-based activities around the coastal areas.

- Wet Season (October to April): - Witnessing the rich and bright sceneries in the Andean highlands and the Amazon jungle.

- Participating in colorful festivals and activities, notably around Carnaval and Semana Santa.

- Discovering the northern coastline archaeological sites, which may have less people.

Other Considerations:

- **Crowds and Tourist Season:** The peak tourist season in Peru corresponds with the dry season from May to September, notably in renowned places like Machu Picchu and Cusco. If you want less visitors, try going during the shoulder seasons (April, October, November) when the weather is still pleasant.

- **Altitude and Acclimatization:** Many of Peru's best attractions are situated at high elevations. To minimise altitude sickness, allow yourself time to adjust by spending a few days in a lower-altitude city like Lima before travelling to higher locations like Cusco.

- Permits and Reservations: Some activities, such as the Inca Trail hike and access to Machu Picchu, need permits that might sell out rapidly, particularly during the high season. It is necessary to plan and schedule these events well in advance.

Chapter 2: Getting to Cusco

the historical and cultural core of Peru, is a vital component of every tourist's visit to this wonderful nation. As the entrance to the famed Machu Picchu and the Sacred Valley, Cusco draws people from all across the globe looking to see its rich Inca legacy, gorgeous scenery, and lively Andean culture. In this detailed guide, we will look into the different transportation choices accessible to travellers, including air travel, land transportation, and practical suggestions for a smooth and comfortable trip to Cusco.

1. By Air:

Cusco's Alejandro Velasco Astete International Airport (CUZ) is the principal aviation hub in the area, linking the city to both local and international destinations. For travellers travelling from remote areas or other countries, flying to Cusco is the most time-efficient and convenient choice.

- **Domestic Flights:** Several airlines, notably LATAM Peru, Avianca Peru, and Sky Airline, provide regular domestic flights to Cusco from Lima, the capital city of Peru, and other significant towns including Arequipa, Juliaca (Puno), and Puerto Maldonado. The flight length from Lima to Cusco is around 1 hour and 20 minutes, making it a short and popular route for passengers.

- **International Flights:** While Cusco's airport mostly handles local flights, there are some international connections available. Direct international flights to Cusco are scarce, although you may find choices from towns like La Paz (Bolivia), Bogotá (Colombia), and Santiago (Chile). Many foreign passengers choose to fly into Lima and then take a local aircraft to Cusco to continue their vacation.

2. Overland Travel: For those preferring a more adventurous and picturesque approach, overland travel to Cusco gives a chance to absorb in the different landscapes and cultures of Peru. There are various common land transportation alternatives available:

- Bus: Peru has an extensive bus network that links major cities and areas. Traveling by bus enables you to observe the shifting sceneries from the coast to the hills. From Lima, the bus travel to Cusco takes roughly 20 to 24 hours, depending on the route and stops. There are also buses from other places, such as Arequipa, Puno, and Nazca, offering flexibility in travel arrangements.

- Train: The Andean Explorer is a luxury train run by Belmond that provides a spectacular and pleasant travel from Cusco to Puno, and vice versa. The route takes you through the gorgeous Andean vistas and delivers outstanding service, making it a wonderful travel experience.

- Self-Drive or Car Rental: For those wishing more freedom, hiring a vehicle and driving to Cusco might be an alternative. However, it's crucial to be aware that roads in Peru may be hard, particularly in hilly places. Additionally, certain distant places may need a 4x4 vehicle.

3. Practical Tips for Travelers:

- Altitude Considerations: Cusco is situated at a high height of roughly 3,400 meters (11,200 feet) above sea level. Altitude sickness is a concern, particularly if travelling from lower elevations. It's vital to take it easy upon arrival, be well-hydrated, and consider acclimatizing for a day or two before indulging in vigorous activities.

- **Travel Insurance:** Before going on your adventure to Cusco, be sure to get comprehensive travel insurance that covers medical emergencies, trip cancellations, and other unforeseen situations. This will give peace of mind and financial protection throughout your travel.

- **Entry Requirements:** Check the visa and entrance requirements for Peru, particularly if you are an international tourist. Most travellers may enter Peru with a valid passport and a tourist visa, which is normally given on arrival.

- **Booking in Advance:** If you intend to visit Machu Picchu or take part in the Inca Trail hike, it's necessary to purchase your tickets and permits well in advance. These famous sites have restricted daily visitor quotas and may sell out rapidly, especially during the busy tourist season.

- **Currency and Payments:** The official currency of Peru is the Peruvian Sol (PEN). While large towns and tourist locations accept credit cards, it's good to carry some cash, particularly for smaller transactions and in more isolated places.

- **Health Precautions:** Before flying to Peru, speak with a healthcare expert about necessary immunisations and health precautions. It's also recommended to bring a basic first-aid kit with vital drugs.

By Air

travelling to Cusco is a popular and easy alternative, and in this guide, we will examine all you need to know about arriving to Cusco by air.

1. Alejandro Velasco Astete International Airport: The Alejandro Velasco Astete International Airport (CUZ) is Cusco's principal air gateway. Located within a short distance from the city center, this airport offers simple access for guests coming by air. It is named for a notable Peruvian aviator and has received extensive renovations over the years to accommodate the expanding number of tourists.

2. Domestic Flights to Cusco: Domestic flights are the most frequent means for Peruvian visitors and travelers from surrounding countries to reach Cusco. Peru's primary carrier, LATAM Airlines Peru (previously known as LAN Peru), and other local airlines run several daily flights linking Cusco with important towns such as Lima, Arequipa, Juliaca, and Puerto Maldonado. These flights provide convenience and efficiency, making it simpler for travellers to experience Cusco's historical monuments and adjacent attractions.

3. International airlines to Cusco: While Cusco is largely serviced by local airlines, there are few international travel alternatives available. Some airlines operate seasonal or charter flights from nearby countries like Bolivia and Chile, catering to passengers wanting direct access to Cusco. However, most foreign visitors choose for a two-step trip, travelling first to Lima's Jorge Chavez foreign Airport (LIM) and then taking a connecting aircraft to Cusco.

4. Lima to Cusco: The Inca Trail via Air:
For many visitors, visiting Cusco is part of a broader adventure that involves climbing the renowned Inca Trail to Machu Picchu. Those visiting from overseas generally arrive in Lima, Peru's capital, and then continue their experience with a flight to Cusco. The Inca

Trail provides a once-in-a-lifetime adventure, exhibiting breathtaking scenery and historic Incan monuments along the route.

5. Altitude Considerations: Cusco's high altitude is something travellers need to consider while travelling to the city. Situated at around 3,400 meters (11,150 feet) above sea level, some tourists may encounter symptoms of altitude sickness, colloquially known as "soroche." To adapt, it is suggested to take it easy upon arriving, remain hydrated, and avoid intense activity for the first day or two.

6. lodgings and Tourism Infrastructure: Cusco provides a broad choice of lodgings catering to varied budgets and interests. From magnificent hotels giving stunning views of the city to small hostels that foster social connections among guests, there is something for everyone. The city's tourist infrastructure has expanded over the years to give guests with a seamless experience, including guided tours, transportation services, and linguistic assistance.

7. Exploring Cusco and Beyond: Once in Cusco, travellers are treated with a multitude of historical and cultural sites. The city's historic core, with its cobblestone streets and well-preserved colonial buildings, is a UNESCO World Heritage Site. Must-visit sights include the Cathedral, the Temple of the Sun (Qoricancha), and the lively San Pedro Market.

Beyond the city, the Sacred Valley beckons with its ancient ruins, quaint towns, and breathtaking views. Many visitors come through the Sacred Valley to explore ancient sites like Pisac and Ollantaytambo, or to start on the renowned train ride to Aguas Calientes, the entrance to Machu Picchu.

8. Sustainable Tourism Initiatives: As the number of visitors visiting Cusco rises, there is a rising focus on sustainable tourism practices. Local authorities and companies are working together to conserve the region's natural and cultural legacy, while also assisting the local residents. Travelers are urged to be responsible tourists by respecting local traditions, limiting their environmental effect, and supporting sustainable tourism efforts.

By Train

While many people come by plane, another popular and beautiful way to see Cusco and its surrounding delights is by rail. Traveling by rail not only gives breathtaking views of the Andean scenery but also allows access to popular attractions like Machu Picchu. In this thorough guide, we will cover all you need to know about experiencing Cusco by rail as a tourist, including train choices, itineraries, tickets, travel recommendations, and more.

1. The PeruRail and Inca Rail Services: The two principal rail services operating in Cusco are PeruRail and Inca Rail. These reputed train companies provide varied routes and services that suit to individual interests and travel schedules.

- PeruRail: PeruRail provides different train services, including the Expedition, Vistadome, and the premium Belmond Hiram Bingham. The Expedition is a comfortable and cost-effective alternative, while the Vistadome gives panoramic windows for a more immersive experience. The Belmond Hiram Bingham provides a luxurious train ride with gourmet meals and live entertainment.

- Inca Rail: Inca Rail offers multiple grades of service, such as the Voyager, the 360°, and the First-Class Executive. The Voyager offers a pleasant and economical ride, the 360°

features panoramic windows, and the First-Class Executive delivers enhanced luxury and amenities.

2. **The Cusco to Machu Picchu Route:** The most renowned rail route in Cusco is the travel to Machu Picchu, the ancient Incan fortress tucked in the Andean highlands. Tourists may take the railway from Cusco or the adjacent town of Ollantaytambo to Aguas Calientes, the base of Machu Picchu.

3. **The Scenic Andean Views:** Traveling by rail from Cusco to Machu Picchu provides a spectacular tour across the Andean landscape. Passengers are exposed to awe-inspiring vistas of verdant valleys, snow-capped mountains, and the trickling Urubamba River, making the train trip a remarkable experience in itself.

4. Tickets and Reservations: To guarantee a pleasant and hassle-free travel, visitors are urged to reserve their train tickets in advance. Tickets may be bought online via the official websites of PeruRail and Inca Rail or through approved travel companies in Cusco. During busy tourist seasons, such as June to August, tickets tend to sell out fast, therefore early booking is encouraged.

5. Train timetable and Duration: The train timetable varies based on the service and route selected. Generally, there are many departures each day from both Cusco and Ollantaytambo to Aguas Calientes. The length of the train travel might vary from around 1.5 to 3.5 hours, depending on the service and stops along the route.

6. Machu Picchu Entrance Tickets: It's crucial for travellers to understand that train tickets do not include access to Machu Picchu itself. Visitors need to acquire separate admission tickets to enter the old citadel. These tickets should also be acquired in advance, particularly during busy tourist seasons.

7. Aguas Calientes: Gateway to Machu Picchu: Upon arriving at Aguas Calientes, travellers may either enjoy the town, take a shuttle bus to Machu Picchu, or start on the difficult climb up to the ancient site. Aguas Calientes includes diverse restaurants, marketplaces, and hot springs, creating a peaceful and colourful setting.

8. The Return Journey: After immersing themselves in the splendour of Machu Picchu, travellers may return to Cusco or other locations by the train. The return ride gives the same spectacular Andean vistas, enabling guests to relish the experience once again before waving goodbye to this amazing site.

9. Sustainable Tourism: As tourism in Cusco continues to increase, ethical travel practices and sustainability are becoming more vital. Tourists are asked to respect local traditions, use designated trails and walkways, and dispose of rubbish respectfully. Train companies like PeruRail and Inca Rail are also pursuing sustainable steps to protect the natural beauty of the area.

By Bus

While many people come by plane or rail, traveling by bus is another popular and adventurous method to enjoy the delights of Cusco and its neighbouring areas. Bus travel gives a unique chance to observe the different landscapes of Peru, engage in the local culture, and visit off-the-beaten-path sites. In this thorough guide, we will cover all the crucial information for travellers touring Cusco by bus, including long-distance buses, local transportation, travel suggestions, and more.

1. Long-Distance Buses to Cusco: Tourists may reach Cusco via long-distance buses from several locations within Peru, including Lima, Arequipa, Puno, and Nazca. Long-distance buses provide an economical and thrilling tour across the different Peruvian landscapes, including the rocky highlands, lush valleys, and the huge altiplano. The bus lines enable guests to enjoy the country's natural splendour while linking to the cultural hub of Cusco.

2. Bus Companies and Services: Peru provides a selection of respectable bus companies that run long-distance services to Cusco. Some well-known firms are Cruz del Sur, Ormeño, and Civa. These bus companies provide varied degrees of service, from ordinary buses to elegant "semi-cama" or "cama" buses with reclining seats, onboard entertainment, and food services.

3. Bus trip Time and Schedule: The trip time to Cusco by long-distance bus varies based on the starting place and route. Travelers from Lima should anticipate a trip of roughly 20 to 24 hours, while those going from towns like Arequipa or Puno can expect shorter travel durations of around 8 to 12 hours. It is essential to verify bus timetables and plan the route properly, particularly during busy tourist seasons.

4. Local Transportation in Cusco: Upon arriving in Cusco, travellers may utilise local transportation alternatives, such as municipal buses and taxis, to traverse the city. City buses provide a cheap method of getting about, with established routes linking different areas and attractions. Taxis are widely accessible and may be hailed from the street or hired via hotels and hostels. It is important to agree on the fee with the taxi driver before commencing the ride.

5. Exploring Cusco and Beyond: Cusco's historical city, a UNESCO World Heritage Site, is best explored on foot, since the tiny cobblestone alleyways are not accessible to automobiles. Tourists may meander through the historic streets, viewing monuments like the Plaza de Armas, the Cathedral, and the Temple of the Sun (Qoricancha). Beyond the city, local buses or excursions may transport travellers to adjacent landmarks, including as the Sacsayhuaman fortress, the Sacred Valley, and Maras-Moray.

6. The Sacred Valley and Beyond: For daring tourists, local buses and excursions allow access to the magnificent Sacred Valley of the Incas. The Sacred Valley is studded with historic sites, mediaeval communities, and colourful marketplaces. Travelers may visit the ancient monuments of Pisac and Ollantaytambo or discover the unusual salt terraces of Maras and the circular agricultural terraces of Moray.

7. Sustainable Tourism: As with any kind of travel, responsible and sustainable tourism practices are crucial. Tourists touring Cusco by bus are advised to respect local customs and traditions, dispose of rubbish correctly, and reduce their environmental effect. Choosing trustworthy bus operators that promote safety and sustainability may also help to responsible travel.

Chapter 3: Exploring Cusco City

situated in the Peruvian Andes, is a city rich in history and culture, noted for its well-preserved colonial architecture and its ancient Inca legacy. As the historic capital of the Inca Empire, Cusco provides a riveting combination of archaeological treasures, bustling marketplaces, and a complex tapestry of cultures. In this thorough guide, we will cover all the crucial information for travellers touring Cusco City, including historical sites, cultural experiences, local food, travel suggestions, and more.

1. The Historical core of Cusco: The historic core of Cusco, a UNESCO World Heritage Site, is the heart of the city and the finest site to start discovering its numerous treasures. The Plaza de Armas, the main plaza, is a focal point surrounded by colonial structures, the

Cathedral, and the Church of La Compañía de Jesús. Tourists may meander through the small cobblestone alleyways, marveling at the beautiful architecture that mixes Inca masonry with Spanish colonial influences.

2. The Cathedral of Santo Domingo: Located on the Plaza de Armas, the Cathedral is a colossal edifice that holds an amazing collection of religious art and relics. Its front exhibits elaborate carvings, and the inside has stunning chapels and altars, making it a notable cultural and religious monument in Cusco.

3. Qoricancha (Temple of the Sun): Qoricancha, formerly the most significant temple in the Inca Empire, is now part of the Santo Domingo Church complex. This archaeological site demonstrates the amazing Inca stone masonry and illustrates the combination of Inca and Spanish architecture.

It is an incredible site to learn about the Inca's religious traditions and their respect for the sun.

4. Sacsayhuaman fortification: Perched on the hills above Cusco, Sacsayhuaman is an impressive Inca fortification that functioned as a military stronghold. The site boasts gigantic stone walls carefully erected without the use of cement, displaying the technical skills of the Incas. Visitors may also enjoy panoramic views of Cusco from this vantage point.

5. San Pedro Market: The busy San Pedro Market is a sensory pleasure, affording an insight into the everyday lives of Cusqueños. Tourists may experience a vivid assortment of fresh fruit, handicrafts, and local cuisines. It's a fantastic spot to try Peruvian street cuisine, purchase souvenirs, and participate with the local culture.

6. Cusco's Culinary Delights: Cusco is a food lover's heaven, with a diversified gourmet scene. Tourists can sample traditional Peruvian cuisine including ceviche, lomo saltado, and alpaca meat. Cusco's food generally contains Andean ingredients, showing a combination of flavors that appeal to varied preferences.

7. Exploring Beyond Cusco: Beyond the city boundaries, travellers may experience the mesmerising sights of the Sacred Valley of the Incas. Pisac and Ollantaytambo are ancient Inca archaeological monuments featuring beautiful terraces and temples. Additionally, Maras and Moray provide unique experiences with their salt mines and circular agricultural terraces.

8. Preparing for the Altitude: Cusco's high altitude of about 3,400 meters (11,150 feet) above sea level might affect certain travellers. To adapt, it is advisable to take it easy upon arrival, remain hydrated, and avoid intense activity for the first day or two. Coca tea, a traditional medicine, is readily accessible and considered to help ease altitude-related symptoms.

9. Local Festivals & Events: Cusco is a city that celebrates its cultural history with several festivals and events throughout the year. Tourists may have the chance to observe colorful processions, traditional dances, and exciting music during these events, offering a unique insight into the local traditions and customs.

10. ethical Tourism: As tourism in Cusco continues to increase, ethical travel habits are crucial to conserving the city's cultural legacy and natural environment. Tourists are asked to respect local traditions, support sustainable efforts, and reduce their environmental effect to preserve the preservation of this magnificent location for future generations.

Plaza de Armas

The Plaza de Armas, commonly known as the Main Square or Plaza Mayor, is a key and historically important place in several towns around Peru. These plazas have served as the core of the city's social, political, and cultural life for centuries, frequently flanked by large colonial structures and showing the architectural fusion of Inca and Spanish influences. In this complete tour, we will concentrate on the Plaza de Armas in Cusco, the historic capital of the Inca Empire and a UNESCO World Heritage Site. As one of the most renowned and dynamic squares in Peru, the Plaza de Armas in Cusco gives travellers a riveting combination of history, architecture, and vivid local culture.

1. Historical Significance of the Plaza de Armas:

The Plaza de Armas in Cusco possesses tremendous historical value, dating back to the period of the Incas. Known as "Huacaypata" or "Aucaypata" in the Inca language, this great plaza was originally the ceremonial and administrative hub of the Inca metropolis. It served as the location for major events, religious rites, and big social gatherings. With the entrance of the Spanish conquistadors in the 16th century, the square underwent metamorphosis into a focus of colonial power, and various Spanish colonial structures were erected around the plaza.

2. Architectural Marvels of the Plaza de Armas:

The Plaza de Armas is flanked by spectacular colonial structures that display the combination of Inca and Spanish architectural styles. The most famous landmark is the Cusco Cathedral, a spectacular example of Spanish Renaissance architecture. The Cathedral's front has beautiful carvings, and its interior holds a rich collection of religious art and antiques, including paintings from the Cusco School, a notable art movement in the area during the colonial period.

Adjacent to the Cathedral lies the Church of La Compañía de Jesús, a remarkable specimen of Baroque architecture. The church's front contains beautiful carvings and complex religious patterns, providing a harmonic combination of Spanish and indigenous culture. Inside, visitors are treated to an exquisite display of gold leaf and magnificent altars, adding to the church's splendour.

At the southeastern corner of the Plaza de Armas, tourists will see the vestiges of the

Inca's Qoricancha, formerly the most significant temple in the Inca Empire. The Spanish eventually erected the Church and Convent of Santo Domingo atop the temple's ruins, resulting in a remarkable blend of Inca masonry and colonial architecture.

3. Cultural Events and Festivities:

The Plaza de Armas is a thriving centre of cultural events and festivals, reflecting the city's vivid traditions and past. Throughout the year, many festivals take place in and around the plaza, encouraging both residents and visitors to join in the city's rich cultural tapestry.

The Inti Raymi festival, celebrated on June 24th, is one of the most major events in Cusco. Also known as the Festival of the Sun, Inti Raymi pays respect to the Inca sun deity, Inti. The event involves colorful processions, traditional dances, and music, culminating in a great finale at the Sacsayhuaman castle, overlooking the city.

4. Gastronomic Delights near the Plaza de Armas:

Surrounding the Plaza de Armas, guests may discover an assortment of restaurants, cafés, and pubs giving a chance to sample wonderful Peruvian food. Whether it's sampling traditional delicacies like ceviche, a delicious meal created from fresh fish marinated in citrus juices, or sipping a cup of rich Peruvian coffee, the Plaza de Armas gives a perfect location to indulge in the country's gastronomic pleasures.

5. Shopping and Souvenirs:

The Plaza de Armas and its nearby lanes are studded with artisanal stores and boutiques where travellers may buy a variety of souvenirs and handicrafts. Items like alpaca wool items, silver jewelry, pottery, and bright fabrics make for fantastic keepsakes of a memorable vacation to Cusco. Tourists may also discover local markets offering a broad selection of handcrafted handicrafts, supporting local craftsmen and communities.

6. People-Watching and Atmosphere:

The Plaza de Armas is a fantastic site for people-watching and soaking in the local ambiance. Tourists may witness inhabitants going about their everyday lives, street entertainers amusing pedestrians, and the occasional traditional Andean music performance. The plaza's dynamic environment offers a feeling of connection with the city and its vibrant culture.

7. Ideal Starting Point for City Exploration:

The Plaza de Armas is conveniently placed in the middle of Cusco, giving it a great starting point for exploring the city's various attractions. From the plaza, travellers may walk through the small cobblestone lanes that connect to various historical sites, museums, and bustling districts. Some important attractions nearby include the San Blas area, the San Pedro Market, and the Santa Catalina Convent.

8. Responsible Tourism near the Plaza de Armas:

As with any tourist location, responsible tourism practices are vital to maintaining the cultural legacy and ecology. Tourists are advised to respect the holy places, follow authorised walkways, and dispose of rubbish respectfully. By patronising local merchants and artists, tourists may contribute positively to the community's economic well-being and the

preservation of the Plaza de Armas as a
beloved monument.

Cusco Cathedral

Nestled in the middle of Cusco's Plaza de
Armas, the Cusco Cathedral is a stunning icon
of colonial architecture and religious legacy.
Also known as the Cathedral Basilica of the
Assumption of the Virgin, this famous
monument serves as a witness to the
combination of Inca and Spanish influences
that define Cusco's cultural diversity. As one of
the most prominent religious and historical
buildings in Peru, Cusco Cathedral attracts
thousands of visitors each year. In this detailed
tour, we will examine the enthralling history,
architectural wonders, precious items, religious
events, visitor experience, and the cultural
relevance of Cusco Cathedral.

1. Historical Background:

Construction of Cusco Cathedral started in 1559, barely a few decades after the Spanish conquistadors landed in the Inca capital. Built on the site of the ancient Inca temple, Qoricancha, the cathedral depicts the Spanish colonial aspirations to demonstrate their cultural and religious authority. The cathedral's construction took over a century to complete, with various adjustments and extensions made throughout the years. Today, it stands as a marvel of colonial architecture, representing a beautiful combination of Renaissance, Baroque, and Andean architectural styles.

2. Architectural Marvels:

Cusco Cathedral's majestic front contains exquisite carvings, sculptural reliefs, and towering bell towers, each demonstrating the workmanship of the Spanish and indigenous artists. The great entryway, embellished with beautiful masonry, is a remarkable example of the Renaissance architecture. As guests enter inside, they are met by a spacious interior area covered with elaborately designed chapels, altars, and holy art.

3. Notable Artifacts and Treasures:

The inside of Cusco Cathedral has an extraordinary collection of religious art and antiques, some of which date back to the colonial period. Notable artefacts include the "Black Christ" picture, known as "El Señor de los Temblores," adored by the people for its protecting abilities against earthquakes. The cathedral is also home to a great collection of religious paintings from the Cusco School, a particular art style that originated during the colonial era.

The High Altar, consisting of finely carved cedar wood, is a magnificent piece of art decorated with silver and gold leaf. It is estimated that around 400 kg of silver were used to embellish the altar. Other remarkable treasures are the magnificent choir stalls, which feature exquisitely carved biblical themes, and the Sacristy, home to a valuable collection of religious costumes and ceremonial relics.

4. Religious Significance:

As a major religious landmark, Cusco Cathedral continues to play a crucial role in the spiritual life of the city. The cathedral serves as the seat of the Archdiocese of Cusco and is the most prominent Catholic temple in the area. It organises many religious rites and processions throughout the year, attracting both committed worshippers and inquisitive visitors alike.

One of the most major religious celebrations is the Corpus Christi procession, celebrated 60 days following Easter Sunday. During this spectacular event, the Cathedral's sacred icons are paraded through the streets of Cusco in a vivid and vibrant demonstration of faith and devotion.

5. Visitor Experience:

Tourists visiting Cusco Cathedral may anticipate a thrilling trip through time and history. Guided tours give thorough insights into the cathedral's design, religious importance, and its role in establishing the cultural environment of Cusco. The beautiful interior, decorated with holy art and gilded altars, puts visitors in awe of the cathedral's magnificence and majesty.

Photography is often permitted within the cathedral, enabling tourists to capture the splendour of the beautiful chapels, altars, and religious artworks. The cathedral also provides an excellent vantage point for panoramic views of the Plaza de Armas and the surrounding city.

6. Preservation Efforts:

Cusco Cathedral's historical and cultural value has led to considerable preservation efforts to conserve its architectural and artistic gems. Conservation measures and continuous maintenance guarantee that this cultural jewel stays intact for future generations to enjoy and love.

7. Cultural Significance:

Beyond its religious significance, Cusco Cathedral bears enormous cultural relevance. It stands as a symbol of the confluence of Inca and Spanish civilizations, illustrating the complicated history of Peru. The cathedral's architectural brilliance and the unique religious artworks inside contribute to Cusco's classification as a UNESCO World Heritage Site.

8. Responsible Tourism:

As with any historical and religious institution, appropriate tourist activities are vital to maintaining Cusco Cathedral's cultural legacy. Tourists are advised to respect the holiness of the area, observe the regulations and instructions set by the cathedral authorities, and avoid disruptive conduct during religious services and activities.

Sacsayhuaman

Nestled high above the city of Cusco in the Peruvian Andes, Sacsayhuaman is a captivating archaeological monument that serves as a witness to the great technical skill and rich history of the Inca civilisation. As one of the most prominent and awe-inspiring Inca ruins in Peru, Sacsayhuaman draws millions of travellers each year, lured by its massive stone walls, exquisite construction, and spectacular panoramic vistas. In this detailed guide, we will dig into the enthralling history, architectural wonders, cultural relevance, visitor experience, and preservation efforts around Sacsayhuaman, delivering an exciting voyage for travellers discovering this ancient wonder.

1. Historical Background:

Sacsayhuaman, known as "sexy-woman," bears tremendous historical value as an ancient Inca citadel and ceremonial site. The name is said to stem from the Quechua words "saqsay" (satisfied or satiated) and "waman" (falcon), indicating the satisfaction or fulfillment enjoyed by the falcon. The site was presumably created during the time of the ninth Inca king, Pachacuti Inca Yupanqui, in the 15th century. Its strategic placement atop a hill overlooking Cusco made it a significant military stronghold and a venue for major religious events.

2. Architectural Marvels:

Sacsayhuaman's most prominent feature is its massive stone walls, erected with an incredible perfection that leaves modern-day spectators in amazement. The castle consists of three large terraced platforms composed of limestone and andesite stones, some weighing up to 200 tons. The stones were painstakingly cut and connected without the use of cement, a stunning feat of engineering that has mystified archaeologists for decades.

The most noticeable element of Sacsayhuaman is the zigzagging walls, which create a vast serpentine structure. This part alone is roughly 360 meters (1,180 feet) long, with walls reaching heights of up to 9 meters (30 feet). The perfection of the stone fitting is so fine that it is stated that not even a piece of paper can fit between the stones.

3. Cultural Significance:

Sacsayhuaman was not just a military fortification but also a location of tremendous religious and cultural value to the Inca civilisation. The elaborate arrangement, ceremonial plazas, and exquisite masonry were thought to depict holy symbols and correlate with celestial events. As a ceremonial location, it saw key rites and religious feasts, notably the celebration of Inti Raymi, the Festival of the Sun, during the winter solstice.

4. Visitor Experience:

Visiting Sacsayhuaman is a transforming experience that enables travellers to journey back in time and observe the architectural brilliance of the Inca civilisation. Tourists may explore the huge terraces, wander along the zigzagging walls, and marvel at the magnificent views of Cusco from the mountaintop. Guided tours give important insights into the site's history, architecture, and cultural importance, offering a fuller knowledge of the Inca's advanced engineering and religious traditions.

The expanse of Sacsayhuaman, along with its ancient stone monuments, creates an unequalled feeling of grandeur and awe, making it a must-visit site for history buffs and cultural travellers alike.

5. Preservation Efforts:

Preserving the integrity of Sacsayhuaman is of vital significance to conserve this priceless cultural treasure for future generations. Ongoing preservation efforts by archaeological professionals and government officials seek to preserve the site's structural integrity and avoid damage caused by natural elements and tourism-related activity.

Tourists are asked to respect the site's sacredness, follow designated walkways, and avoid from touching or climbing on the old stone walls to preserve the fragile masonry. Responsible tourist activities are vital to safeguard the survival of Sacsayhuaman's architectural wonders.

6. Trekking and Alternative Routes:

In addition to the main entrance accessible by road, adventurous travellers may also select for hiking paths that go to Sacsayhuaman. One famous walk is the short but steep ascent from Cusco via the San Cristobal district, affording spectacular views of the city and the surrounding environment.

Another alternate path is the lengthier but spectacular journey known as the "Cusco 3 Balconies Walk." This journey traverses via three hilltop viewpoints—Tambomachay, Puka Pukara, and Q'enqo—before concluding at Sacsayhuaman. This approach gives a unique view on Cusco's terrain and the strategic location of these historic landmarks.

7. Photography and Souvenirs:

Photography is permitted inside Sacsayhuaman, giving travellers with the chance to photograph the site's breathtaking splendour and the surrounding nature. Visitors may take home enduring recollections of their interaction with the Inca's architectural treasures.

Additionally, several vendors at the entry provide a selection of handicrafts, fabrics, and souvenirs produced by local craftsmen.

Purchasing these things helps support the local community and aids to the preservation of the cultural history in the area.

8. Responsible Tourism:

To preserve the preservation of Sacsayhuaman for centuries to come, appropriate tourist practices are necessary. Tourists are asked to preserve the site's sacredness, follow specified walkways, and avoid touching or climbing on the old stone walls. Littering should be avoided, and any garbage should be disposed of correctly.

Qorikancha (Temple of the Sun)

Qorikancha, commonly known as the Temple of the Sun, is a religious and historically important landmark situated in the centre of

Cusco, Peru. As one of the most venerated temples of the Inca Empire, Qorikancha retains a great spiritual and cultural importance. The name "Qorikancha" originates from the Quechua words "quri" (gold) and "kancha" (enclosure), translating to "Golden Enclosure." In this detailed guide, we will explore into the enthralling history, architectural wonders, religious and cultural value, visitor experience, and preservation efforts around Qorikancha, delivering an exciting voyage for travellers discovering this ancient masterpiece.

1. Historical Background:

Qorikancha's history extends back to the early days of the Inca Empire when it functioned as the most prominent sacred site and a monument to the sun deity, Inti. The temple was established during the time of the ninth Inca monarch, Pachacuti Inca Yupanqui, who rebuilt and renovated the site to worship Inti as the primary god. Qorikancha had a significant part in Inca religious life, providing as a venue for rites, ceremonies, and astronomical observations.

With the entrance of the Spanish conquistadors in the 16th century, Qorikancha witnessed a tremendous alteration. The Spanish erected the Church and Convent of Santo Domingo upon the Inca temple's foundations, using the stones from the original construction. This mix of Inca stonework and Spanish colonial buildings has produced a unique and awe-inspiring fusion of civilizations.

2. Architectural Marvels:

Qorikancha's initial structure is thought to have been a brilliant exhibition of Inca design and engineering. The walls were built with precision, showing the Inca's excellent masonry talents. The temple's foundations were erected utilising enormous stones cut and fitted together without the use of cement, a hallmark feature of Inca building.

The temple complex comprised of many rooms and courtyards, each fulfilling unique religious and ceremonial functions. The centre courtyard, known as the Sun Courtyard, had a gilded image of the sun, where priests and nobles would meet to pay tribute to Inti. The temple's construction was built to line with the solstices and equinoxes, further underlining the importance of astronomical observations in Inca religious beliefs.

3. Religious and Cultural Significance:

Qorikancha possessed tremendous religious and cultural value to the Inca culture. The temple was considered the most holy and venerated location in the Inca Empire, reflecting the divine link between the king, the gods, and the people. It was devoted to Inti, the sun deity, who symbolised life, fertility, and wealth.

Qorikancha played a prominent part in several religious rites, including sacrifices to Inti, agricultural festivals, and celebrations of solstices and equinoxes. The temple's construction and placement were considered to enable a harmonious link between the heavenly world and the terrestrial realm.

4. Visitor Experience:

For visitors, a visit to Qorikancha is a deep and transformational experience, affording a look into the spiritual and cultural history of the Inca civilisation. The restored pieces of Inca masonry with the majestic colonial architecture of Santo Domingo Church give a rare chance to observe the blending of two separate civilizations.

Guided tours are provided to give deep insights into the history, architecture, and religious importance of Qorikancha. Visitors may visit the well-preserved rooms, courtyards, and shrines, learning about the rites and ceremonies that formerly took place inside these hallowed walls.

The Sun Courtyard, decked with gold during the Inca Empire, is a particularly attractive portion of the temple complex. Although the original gold items are no longer visible, the importance of this location as a spiritual center remains tangible.

5. Preservation Efforts:

Preserving Qorikancha is of crucial significance to conserve this priceless cultural and historical legacy for future generations. Archaeological specialists and government officials work carefully to preserve the site's structural integrity and safeguard it from damage caused by natural elements and tourism-related activities.

Visitors are asked to preserve the holiness of Qorikancha and follow the prescribed walkways to minimise excessive pressure on the old stones. Guided tours guarantee that guests obtain correct information while minimizing any harmful influence on the site's conservation.

6. Cultural Context and Reverence:

Qorikancha continues to possess cultural value and is a holy location for Andean tribes. The rites and ceremonies honoring Inti and Pachamama (Mother Earth) continue to be done by local communities, linking the present with the ancient past.

Throughout the year, notably during the Inti Raymi festival, Qorikancha is a focal place for spiritual meetings and offerings, inviting both residents and visitors alike to partake in the celebration of Andean customs.

7. Photography and Souvenirs:

Photography is permitted inside Qorikancha, giving travellers with the chance to photograph the site's unique combination of Inca and Spanish construction. Capturing the beauty of the Sun Courtyard and the beautiful stones is a fantastic way to keep the memories of this historical masterpiece.

Near the entrance of Qorikancha, tourists may discover artisanal stores and vendors providing a selection of handicrafts, fabrics, and gifts. Purchasing these things benefits the local community and aids to the preservation of cultural heritage in the area.

8. Responsible Tourism:

Responsible tourist practices are crucial to maintain the preservation of Qorikancha's cultural and historical value. Tourists are requested to obey the rules established by the site management, respect designated areas, and avoid from touching or climbing on the old stones. Additionally, littering should be minimised, and any garbage should be disposed of correctly.

San Pedro Market

San Pedro Market, called locally as "Mercado de San Pedro," is a colourful and busy market situated in Cusco, Peru. As one of the city's oldest and most prominent marketplaces, it bears tremendous cultural value and provides travellers a riveting glimpse into the daily lives of Cusco's citizens. The market is not only a centre for shopping but also a cultural event, where residents and tourists come together to trade items, eat traditional food, and immerse themselves in the rich legacy of Peru. In this thorough guide, we will cover the history, goods and offers, cultural importance, tourist experience, and responsible tourism practices around San Pedro Market.

1. Historical Background:

San Pedro Market has a rich and colourful history, extending back to pre-colonial times when it was a key trade site for the Inca Empire. The market's position near the old Inca city of Cusco made it a vital economic centre, where items from diverse parts of the empire were brought for trade.

After the Spanish conquistadors came in the 16th century, the market continued to develop and evolved into its current shape. Over the ages, it has expanded in size and breadth, adjusting to the changing requirements of the local population and becoming a thriving hub of trade and culture in Cusco.

2. Products and Offerings:

San Pedro Market is a treasure trove of commodities, providing an astounding selection of things that appeal to both residents and visitors. The market is separated into sections, each specialised in various things, offering a colourful and diversified shopping experience.

a. Fresh Produce: One of the primary attractions of the market is its range of fresh fruits and vegetables. Visitors may discover a broad range of locally produced products, including exotic fruits specific to the Andean area.

b. Handicrafts and fabrics: San Pedro Market is a sanctuary for handicraft connoisseurs, providing a large choice of traditional Peruvian fabrics, alpaca wool goods, ceramics, and delicately created souvenirs.

c. Food & Beverages: The market is a gourmet feast, with several food booths and cafes giving a taste of real Peruvian cuisine. From ceviche and empanadas to chicha morada (purple corn drink), tourists may taste the unique cuisines of Peru.

d. Herbs and Medicinal Plants: Another intriguing segment of the market is the one devoted to traditional medicine. Local sellers offer numerous herbs and medicinal plants, many of which have been utilised for millennia by indigenous people for their curative powers.

e. Andean Products: San Pedro Market is a terrific opportunity to explore Andean specialities, such quinoa, kiwicha (amaranth), coca leaves, and several sorts of potatoes.

3. Cultural Significance:

San Pedro Market plays a key role in conserving and promoting Peru's cultural history. The market is a colourful melting pot of customs, where travellers may connect with people, learn about their way of life, and develop a greater appreciation of Peruvian culture.

The market's concentration on locally produced items and traditional crafts helps and preserves the lives of local craftsmen and farmers. The bright fabrics and handicrafts on show represent the creative abilities handed down through generations, expressing the Andean people' strong cultural identity.

4. Visitor Experience:

Visiting San Pedro Market is an interesting and engaging experience for travellers. Exploring the market's convoluted lanes and kiosks gives a real view into the everyday lives of Cusco's citizens.

The busy environment, brilliant colors, and fragrant fragrances create a sensory explosion that immerses visitors in the varied tapestry of Peruvian culture. Engaging with local merchants, sampling samples of rare fruits, and bartering for gifts adds to the distinct and real experience of the market.

5. Responsible Tourism:

Responsible tourist practices are vital to promote the survival of San Pedro Market and its cultural heritage. Tourists are recommended to respect the local customs and traditions, abstain from bartering unduly, and buy things directly from local merchants wherever feasible.

Avoiding single-use plastic and disposing of garbage ethically are vital to limit the market's environmental effect. As San Pedro Market is a vital cultural area, visitors are asked to be courteous and thoughtful when taking pictures.

6. Location and Accessibility:

San Pedro Market is strategically placed in Cusco's Plaza de Armas, making it readily accessible to travellers exploring the city's historical monuments. It is a perfect starting place for a cultural trip in Cusco, giving insight into the city's history, present, and dynamic local life.

7. Preserving Traditional Practices:

San Pedro Market acts as a venue for maintaining traditional customs and knowledge. Visitors may observe craftsmen and traders effectively performing their skills and learn about the cultural importance of their items. Supporting these traditional traditions via responsible tourism helps protect Peru's cultural heritage and fosters the continuance of time-honored rituals.

Museums and Art Galleries

Peru, a region of ancient civilizations and rich cultural history, provides a profusion of museums and art galleries that capture the hearts of interested tourists. From pre-Columbian antiquities to modern masterpieces, the nation shows a vast variety of art and history. In this thorough guide, we'll take you on a tour of some of the most spectacular museums and art galleries in Peru, enabling you to dive deep into the nation's history, artistry, and customs.

1. Museo Larco - Lima:

Located in the capital city, Lima, Museo Larco is a must-visit museum for every art and history aficionado. It holds a vast collection of pre-Columbian art and antiquities, including ceramics, textiles, jewelry, and ancient earthenware. The museum's superbly maintained exhibits give insights into the interesting civilizations that existed in ancient Peru.

2. Museo Nacional de Arqueología, Antropología e Historia del Perú - Lima:

Also located in Lima, the Museo Nacional de Arqueología, Antropología e Historia del Perú is the country's most major archaeological museum. It shows an astonishing assortment of artifacts from numerous pre-Inca and Inca civilizations, offering an insight into the country's complex history.

3. Museo de Arte de Lima (MALI) - Lima:

Art fans will be charmed with the Museo de Arte de Lima (MALI), devoted to Peruvian art dating from colonial periods to the current age. The museum's enormous collection comprises paintings, sculptures, and modern art, presenting an aesthetic journey through Peru's history.

4. Museo de Arte Contemporáneo (MAC) - Lima:

For those seeking contemporary art experiences, the Museo de Arte Contemporáneo (MAC) in Lima gives a new view into Peru's current art scene. Featuring rotating exhibits of prominent artists, this museum honours the country's modern creative manifestations.

5. Museo Nacional de la Cultura Peruana - Lima:

To grasp the cultural richness of Peru, a visit to the Museo Nacional de la Cultura Peruana is vital. This museum shows traditional Peruvian art, crafts, and costumes, emphasising the country's unique tapestry of cultures and beliefs.

6. Museo Tumbas Reales de Sipán - Lambayeque:

Located in Lambayeque, northern Peru, Museo Tumbas Reales de Sipán is an archaeological jewel devoted to the Moche civilisation. Visitors may marvel at the ornate tomb of the Lord of Sipán, which contains fine gold and silver objects, allowing an insight into ancient royal life.

7. Museo Nacional de Sicán - Lambayeque:

Adjacent to the Tumbas Reales de Sipán, the Museo Nacional de Sicán concentrates on the lesser-known Sicán civilisation. The museum shows amazing relics, including fine metalwork and ceramics, offering insight on this unique pre-Inca civilisation.

8. Museo de Sitio Manuel Chávez Ballón - Machu Picchu:

While seeing the historic Inca fortress of Machu Picchu, make sure to visit the Museo de Sitio Manuel Chávez Ballón. This museum gives context to the site's history and offers a fuller knowledge of the Inca culture that once thrived there.

9. Museo Amano - Lima:

For those captivated by textiles and materials, the Museo Amano in Lima offers an excellent collection of pre-Columbian textiles. The museum's displays illustrate the ancient skill of weaving and the importance of textiles in Peruvian culture.

10. Museo Pedro de Osma - Lima:

Housed in a lovely colonial home, the Museo Pedro de Osma showcases a spectacular collection of colonial art, including paintings, sculptures, and decorative arts. This museum gives a unique viewpoint on Peru's colonial history and artistic influences

Chapter 4: Sacred Valley of the Incas

The Sacred Valley of the Incas in Peru is a stunning and captivating site that captivates people from all over the globe. Nestled in the Andes highlands, this valley offers great historical and cultural value since it was originally the centre of the Inca Empire. With its magnificent scenery, historic ruins, and active local communities, the Sacred Valley provides a unique and remarkable experience for travellers looking to see the marvels of Peru.

1. Introduction to the Sacred Valley of the Incas:

The Sacred Valley, also known as Urubamba Valley, spans from the settlement of Pisac to the ancient Inca city of Machu Picchu. It functioned as a vital agricultural zone for the

Incas owing to its good soil and mild temperature. Today, the valley remains as a tribute to the excellent engineering and architectural talents of the Inca civilisation, with well-preserved ruins and terraces that elegantly fit into the natural surroundings.

2. Getting to the Sacred Valley: The major entry to the Sacred Valley is via Cusco, the ancient capital of the Inca Empire. Tourists may reach Cusco by Alejandro Velasco Astete International Airport or by rail from major Peruvian cities. From Cusco, the Sacred Valley is accessible by road, providing spectacular travels through stunning scenery.

3. Top Attractions in the Sacred Valley:

a. Pisac: This lovely community is famed for its thriving artisan market and the old Inca ruins atop the hill, displaying outstanding agricultural terraces and ceremonial structures.

a. Ollantaytambo: An Inca stronghold with enormous stone walls and complex stone masonry, Ollantaytambo gives an insight into the strategic military architecture of the Incas.

c. Maras Salt Ponds: The unique salt evaporation ponds in Maras have been utilised since pre-Inca times, and tourists may see the salt extraction process and buy high-quality salt goods.

d. Moray: An agricultural experimental hub of the Incas, Moray boasts circular terraces of varied microclimates, exhibiting the genius of Inca agricultural operations.

e. Chinchero: This traditional Andean community is known for its genuine textile manufacture, and tourists may observe the weaving process and buy stunning handmade textiles.

f. Urubamba: Known as the "Heart of the Sacred Valley," this town has a central position and serves as a base for visiting the surrounding sights.

4. The Majestic Machu Picchu: While not exactly part of the Sacred Valley, no tour would be complete without mentioning Machu Picchu. Accessible by rail or walking, this UNESCO World Heritage Site is a famous emblem of the Inca civilisation and draws millions of tourists each year.

5. Outdoor Activities and Adventure: For nature aficionados and adventure seekers, the Sacred Valley provides a wealth of thrilling activities. From hiking and trekking along historic Inca paths to white-water rafting in the Urubamba River, the valley gives opportunity for adrenaline-pumping excursions among breathtaking natural settings.

6. Cultural Immersion and Local people: Interacting with the local people is a highlight of visiting the Sacred Valley. Travelers may participate in real Andean rites, enjoy traditional festivals, and learn about the rich cultural legacy of the area.

7. Gastronomy in the Sacred Valley: Peruvian food is known internationally, and the Sacred Valley is no exception. Visitors may experience wonderful traditional meals created from locally-sourced ingredients, including maize, potatoes, and a range of meats. Don't miss the opportunity to sample the renowned Peruvian cuisine, "Cuy" (guinea pig).

8. Best Time to Visit: The Sacred Valley may be visited year-round, although the optimal time is during the dry season from April to October. This season provides sunny sky and temperate temperatures, making it great for touring the ancient sites and enjoying outdoor activities.

9. Responsible Tourism and Sustainability: As the Sacred Valley receives a growing number of visitors, it is necessary to encourage responsible tourism practices. Supporting local craftspeople, appreciating the cultural legacy, and being sensitive of the environment are crucial to maintaining the valley's beauty for future generations.

Pisac

Pisac, a charming community in the Sacred Valley of the Incas, Peru, is a hidden jewel that entices guests with its rich history, colourful culture, and stunning views. This thorough book seeks to give travellers with an in-depth insight of Pisac, its major attractions, outdoor activities, local customs, and practical travel suggestions for an enjoyable trip.

1. Introduction to Pisac: Nestled at the foot of the Andes mountains, Pisac is situated approximately 35 kilometers from Cusco, making it conveniently accessible for travellers touring the Sacred Valley. The community is famed for its well-preserved Inca ruins, lovely colonial architecture, and a busy crafts market that draws people from across the globe.

2. The Archaeological Site of Pisac:

a. Pisac Ruins: The old Inca fortress built high on a mountain crest overlooks the settlement. It functioned as a key military fortification and ceremonial place. The well-preserved agricultural terraces display Inca technical prowess, and the Temple of the Sun and Intihuatana (hitching post of the sun) are exceptional architectural accomplishments.

b. Q'allaqasa: Situated on the other side of the valley, Q'allaqasa is a lesser-known archaeological site comprising tiered platforms and old houses. The location provides spectacular panoramic views of Pisac and the adjacent valley.

3. Exploring the Village of Pisac:

a. Pisac Market: The colorful handcraft market conducted on Tuesdays, Thursdays, and Sundays is a must-visit site. Local craftsmen showcase a varied assortment of textiles, pottery, jewelry, and traditional Andean handicrafts, making it a wonderful spot to acquire unique mementos.

b. San Pedro Church: The lovely colonial-era church is in the main plaza and features an elaborately carved façade. Visitors may appreciate the blend of Inca and Spanish architectural elements within the church.

c. Pisac Cemetery: Situated on a neighbouring hill, the pre-Columbian cemetery displays ancient graves cut into the rocks. It gives insights into the burial traditions and beliefs of the Incas.

4. Outdoor Activities and Adventure:

a. Hiking to the Pisac Ruins: Trekking to the Pisac Ruins is a wonderful experience, giving spectacular views of the valley and a chance to immerse in nature. There are several hiking paths of varying difficulty levels appealing to all sorts of travellers.

b. riding trips: Explore the Sacred Valley on two wheels with guided riding trips that take you through stunning scenery and quaint communities, presenting a unique view of the area.

c. Paragliding: For adrenaline addicts, paragliding above the Sacred Valley provides a thrilling flying experience and spectacular panoramas of the highlands and the Pisac Ruins.

d. Rafting: The Urubamba River offers exhilarating white-water rafting options, excellent for anyone wanting an adventure on the water.

5. native Traditions & Cultural Experiences:

a. Andean rituals: Engage in real Andean rituals lead by native shamans, giving a spiritual and cultural connection with the ancient traditions of the Andes.

b. Pisac Festivals: If your visit coincides with local festivals, such as the Inti Raymi (Festival of the Sun) or Virgen del Carmen, you'll see vivid parades, music, dancing, and traditional rituals that commemorate the region's cultural history.

6. Gastronomy in Pisac: Delight your taste buds with the delicacies of Peruvian cuisine in the village's local cafes. Try traditional delicacies like "Cuy al Horno" (roasted guinea pig) or relish a range of Andean specialities crafted from locally-sourced ingredients.

7. greatest Time to Visit Pisac: The dry season from April to October is the greatest time to visit Pisac, giving good weather and clear sky. However, Pisac's splendour shines year-round, and even during the rainy season (November to March), the terrain stays rich and appealing.

8. lodging & Lodging: Pisac provides a choice of lodging alternatives, from modest guesthouses and boutique hotels to lovely lodges that mix well with the natural surroundings. Staying in Pisac enables guests to immerse themselves in the local culture and experience the quiet ambiance of the valley.

9. Responsible Tourism and Sustainability: As tourism expands in Pisac, it is necessary to practice responsible travel to conserve the environment, help local people, and maintain the cultural history of the area. Engaging in sustainable tourism projects and honouring local traditions are key steps in ensuring Pisac remains an amazing destination for decades to come.

Ollantaytambo

Ollantaytambo, an old Inca citadel and settlement situated in the Sacred Valley of the Incas, Peru, is a mesmerising site that provides a unique combination of history, architecture, and natural beauty. This thorough book seeks to give travellers with an in-depth overview of Ollantaytambo, its key attractions, historical importance, outdoor activities, local culture, and practical travel suggestions for a great trip.

1. Introduction to Ollantaytambo:

Nestled amid the foothills of the Andes mountains, Ollantaytambo is roughly 60 kilometers northwest of Cusco and serves as a vital location along the Inca Trail leading to Machu Picchu. With its well-preserved Inca ruins and picturesque cobblestone alleys, Ollantaytambo gives a look into the brilliant engineering and urban planning of the Inca civilisation.

2. The Archaeological Site of Ollantaytambo:

a. Ollantaytambo fortification: The primary feature of the hamlet is the Ollantaytambo Fortress, an astonishing complex of stone constructions that functioned as both a ceremonial center and a defensive fortification. The site boasts gigantic stone walls, complicated terraces, and a sophisticated irrigation system that demonstrates the outstanding architectural talents of the Incas.

b. Temple of the Sun: Within the stronghold, the Temple of the Sun shows exquisitely sculpted stonework, including six huge monoliths that were designed to depict the Inca gods and astronomical observations.

c. Terraces of Pumatallis: Situated on the hill opposite the citadel, these agricultural terraces give stunning views of the settlement and surrounding valley.

3. Exploring the Village of Ollantaytambo:

a. Ollantaytambo square: The centre of the settlement is the main square, flanked by well-preserved Inca walls and colonial-style houses. It is a wonderful site to immerse in the local culture and watch the everyday lives of the locals.

b. Ollantaytambo Market: The local market, held on Sundays, Tuesdays, and Thursdays, provides a variety of handicrafts, textiles, and local products, making it an ideal spot to buy souvenirs and mingle with the friendly inhabitants.

c. Pinkuylluna Mountain Granaries: Hiking up to the Pinkuylluna granaries enables tourists to examine ancient storehouses constructed into the hillside, offering insight into the Inca agricultural and storage activities.

4. Historical Significance of Ollantaytambo:
a. Inca fight: Ollantaytambo played a key part in the Inca fight against Spanish invasion. The fortification functioned as a bastion during the final Inca revolt headed by Manco Inca Yupanqui, displaying the strategic military superiority of the Incas.

a. Living Inca Town: Unlike many other Inca sites that were abandoned or destroyed following the Spanish conquest, Ollantaytambo has continued to be inhabited since the Inca period, giving it a living witness to the region's rich history.

5. Outdoor Activities and Adventure:

a. Hiking and hiking: Ollantaytambo serves as a starting point for many hiking routes, including the famed Inca Trail leading to Machu Picchu. Additionally, guests may explore neighbouring trails and appreciate the picturesque splendour of the Sacred Valley.

b. bicycling trips: Guided bicycling trips allow guests to explore the surrounding countryside, giving opportunity to connect with local people and experience traditional Andean life.

c. Climbing: Adventure enthusiasts may join in rock climbing activities in the adjacent mountains, delivering a thrilling experience among stunning views.

6. Local Culture and Traditions: a. Festivals and Celebrations: If your visit corresponds with local festivals, such as the Raymi celebration, you'll have the opportunity to see colorful processions, traditional dances, and bright celebrations that commemorate Inca history and local traditions.

a. Chicherías: Ollantaytambo is noted for its traditional chicherías, local pubs where tourists can drink "chicha," a traditional fermented corn liquor popular since Inca times.

7. Gastronomy in Ollantaytambo: Sample the tastes of Peruvian cuisine in the village's restaurants and cafes, offering a mix of traditional meals and foreign selections. Don't miss eating local specialties like "Pachamanca," a typical Andean meal baked in a subterranean oven.

8. greatest Time to Visit Ollantaytambo: The dry season from April to October is the greatest time to visit Ollantaytambo, giving beautiful weather and clear sky for touring the ancient site and enjoying outdoor activities. However, Ollantaytambo's attractiveness persists throughout the year, with its lush vegetation during the rainy season (November to March) bringing a new type of enchantment.

9. lodging & Lodging: Ollantaytambo provides a choice of lodging alternatives, from comfortable hostels and boutique hotels to eco-lodges that fit well with the natural surroundings. Staying in the village enables guests to enjoy its unique charm and kindness.

10. Practical Travel Tips:

a. height: Ollantaytambo is at a height of roughly 2,800 meters (9,186 feet) above sea level. It is suggested to acclimatize at Cusco or a lower-altitude place before going to minimise altitude-related discomfort.

b. Tickets and Passes: To explore the Ollantaytambo ancient site and other adjacent attractions, travellers may require a "Boleto Turístico del Cusco" (Cusco Tourist Ticket) or particular admission tickets, depending on the locations they desire to visit.

c. Machu Picchu Connection: Ollantaytambo serves as a starting point for the railway trip to Machu Picchu. Tourists wishing to visit the renowned fortress should buy train tickets and Machu Picchu admission tickets well in advance.

Moray

Moray, a mysterious and awe-inspiring archaeological site situated in the Sacred Valley of the Incas, Peru, is a riveting location that draws travellers with its unusual circular terraces and old agricultural experimental center. This thorough book seeks to offer travellers with an in-depth overview of Moray, its historical significance, geological wonder, cultural relevance, outdoor activities, and practical travel suggestions for a memorable and instructive stay.

1. Introduction to Moray: Situated around 50 kilometers northwest of Cusco, Moray is an intriguing site that serves as a witness to the remarkable architectural and agricultural abilities of the Inca civilisation. The site features many circular terraces constructed into a natural dip in the earth, producing a magnificent amphitheater-like configuration. Moray's purpose and the mystery surrounding its creation continue to attract the interest of people from throughout the globe.

2. The Historical Significance of Moray:

a. Agricultural Experimentation: Scholars think that Moray acted as an agricultural experiment for the Incas. The circular terraces are thought to have been used to raise a broad range of crops, with each level replicating distinct microclimates. The Incas employed this creative technique to discover ideal growth conditions for diverse crops, leading to their capacity to support vast populations across the empire.

b. Religious and Ritualistic Importance: Some ideas imply that Moray possessed spiritual value for the Incas, acting as a place for religious events or rituals to honor their agricultural deities. The site's distinctive layout and link with the surrounding terrain may have been viewed as holy by the ancient Inca culture.

3. The Geological Marvel of Moray: The design and building of Moray are a tribute to the Incas' excellent grasp of geology and engineering. The circular terraces provide a succession of temperature fluctuations between each level, which vary up to 27°F (15°C). The temperature variance enabled the Incas to examine crops' resilience to various elevations and climatic conditions.

4. Exploring the Moray Archaeological Site: Visiting Moray gives a rare chance to observe historic agricultural ingenuity and immerse in the history of the Inca civilisation.

a. Circular Terraces: The major feature of Moray is the succession of concentric circular terraces, each varying in size and depth. Descending onto the terraces, tourists may explore and enjoy the architectural wonder that is still present after centuries.

b. Amphitheater-like Formation: As visitors stroll up the terraces, they'll note the site's uncanny similarity to an amphitheater, adding to its mystery and attraction.

c. Interpretive Signage: Informational boards installed at the site give significant insights about Moray's history, the Inca's farming techniques, and the value of this unique archaeological marvel.

5. Outdoor Activities and Adventure: a. Trekking: Hiking to Moray from adjacent settlements or as part of an organised trip lets guests to observe the spectacular Andean sceneries and take in the breathtaking vistas of the surrounding mountains and valleys.

a. Mountain bike: Cycling enthusiasts can go on guided mountain bike trips through the picturesque countryside, delivering a thrilling and immersive experience of the Sacred Valley.

6. Local Culture and Community Interaction: Visiting Moray gives a chance to meet with the local inhabitants and learn about their cultural history and agricultural customs. Engaging with the people gives insights into the region's everyday life, culinary customs, and traditional crafts.

7. greatest Time to Visit Moray: The dry season from April to October is the greatest time to visit Moray, giving clear sky and excellent weather for exploring the site and enjoying outdoor activities. However, Moray's beauty is mesmerising throughout the year, and even during the rainy season (November to March), the terraces keep their unique attractiveness.

8. Nearby Attractions: Tourists visiting Moray may explore other key sites in the Sacred Valley, such as Maras Salt Ponds, Pisac Ruins, and Ollantaytambo, which are all reasonably accessible from Moray and give a fuller insight of the Inca civilisation.

9. Practical Travel Tips: a. height: Moray is situated at a reasonably high height of roughly 3,500 meters (11,483 feet) above sea level. To acclimatize, it is advised to spend a few days in Cusco or a lower-altitude place before visiting Moray.

a. Tickets and Passes: To enter Moray, tourists may require a "Boleto Turístico del Cusco" (Cusco Tourist Ticket), which covers entry to Moray and other surrounding archaeological sites.

Maras Salt Mines

Maras Salt Mines, a captivating and historically important monument situated in the Sacred Valley of the Incas, Peru, is a unique location that amazes travellers with its ancient salt evaporation ponds and traditional salt harvesting techniques. This comprehensive book seeks to give travellers with an in-depth overview of the Maras Salt Mines, its historical background, geological wonder, cultural relevance, visiting experiences, outdoor activities, and practical travel suggestions for a memorable and instructive vacation.

1. Introduction to Maras Salt Mines:

Situated around 48 kilometers northwest of Cusco, the Maras Salt Mines, also known as Salineras de Maras, are a complex system of salt evaporation ponds going back to pre-Inca times. These intriguing salt terraces have been in constant use for millennia and serve as a tribute to the excellent agricultural and technical skills of the ancient civilizations in the area.

2. The Historical Background of Maras Salt Mines:

a. Pre-Inca Origins: The history of the Maras Salt Mines extends back well before the Inca civilisation. The salt extraction processes utilised in Maras have been dated back to the Wari civilisation, which lived between 500 and 1000 AD.

b. Inca Influence: During the Inca Empire, the location was extensively expanded, and the salt manufacturing technologies were enhanced. The Incas utilised the salt for preserving food and as a lucrative commercial item.

c. Continued custom: The custom of salt harvesting has been handed down through centuries, and even today, local families maintain the ponds and participate in the salt extraction process.

3. The Geological Marvel of Maras Salt Mines:

a. Natural Saltwater Springs: The salt evaporation ponds of Maras are supplied by a natural saltwater spring that originates from the slope. The high mineral concentration of the water, including sodium chloride and other minerals, adds to the peculiar flavour and quality of the salt produced.

b. Terraced Salt Ponds: The saltwater is funnelled into a network of delicately terraced ponds, which vary in size and depth. As the water evaporates under the intense Andean sun, the salt crystallizes on the pond surface, finally reaching the appropriate level of concentration.

c. Shimmering White Salt Crusts: The outcome of this procedure is a spectacular sight of gleaming white salt crusts that cover the ponds, producing a visually breathtaking scene.

4. Exploring the Maras Salt Mines: Visiting the Maras Salt Mines provides travellers an immersive experience in the salt harvesting practises and a chance to observe the natural beauty of the tiered ponds.

a. Walking Tour: Visitors may join a guided walking tour to see the salt mines and learn about the traditional ways of salt extraction. Local guides share insights into the history, culture, and processes of the salt industry.

b. Viewing Platforms: Several viewing platforms are strategically positioned throughout the site, giving panoramic views of the salt terraces and the surrounding valley.

c. Interacting with Local Salt Workers: Engaging with the local families working in the salt mines gives a chance to learn their daily routines and the relevance of salt production to their lives.

5. Cultural Importance of Maras Salt Mines:

a. Traditional history: The salt harvesting techniques employed in Maras have been conserved for generations and are strongly rooted in the cultural history of the local inhabitants. The continuance of this historic custom displays the commitment and respect for their elders' knowledge and habits.

b. Socio-Economic Impact: The salt production in Maras contributes significantly to the local economy, providing livelihoods for the families involved in the salt harvesting process and generating money through tourism.

6. Outdoor Activities and Adventure:

a. Moray and Maras Salt Mines Tour: Many tours offer combined excursions to Moray and the Maras Salt Mines, enabling travellers to see two remarkable ancient sites in the same trip.

b. Hiking and Trekking: For nature aficionados, there are hiking and trekking options in the surrounding region, affording stunning views of the Andean scenery and the Sacred Valley.

7. finest Time to Visit Maras Salt Mines: The dry season from April to October is the finest time to visit the Maras Salt Mines, since the weather is comfortable, and the salt terraces are at their most brilliant condition. However, the place is available year-round, and even during the rainy season (November to March), visitors may still experience the unique beauty of the salt ponds.

8. Practical Travel Tips:

a. courteous Photography: While photography is permitted, it is crucial to be courteous to the local employees and their privacy. Always ask for permission before shooting close-up shots of folks.

b. Salt keepsakes: Visitors may buy bags of locally harvested salt as keepsakes. Supporting the local economy via buying salt goods helps support this ancient sector.

c. height: Maras is located at a height of roughly 3,380 meters (11,089 feet) above sea level. Tourists should acclimatize at Cusco or a lower-altitude region before going to minimise altitude-related discomfort.

9. Sustainable Tourism and Responsible Travel:

a. Conservation Efforts: As Maras Salt Mines draw more visitors, it is necessary to encourage responsible tourism practices to maintain the site's natural beauty and cultural value. Visitors should avoid from polluting and respect the local ecosystem.

b. Support Local Community: Engaging in the local economy via guided tours, buying souvenirs, and honouring the customs of the salt workers helps support the local community and assures the sustainable preservation of this cultural asset.

Chapter 5: Machu Picchu

Machu Picchu, the legendary Inca citadel situated in the Andes mountains of Peru, is a bucket-list destination for travellers eager to experience the grandeur of ancient civilizations and immerse themselves in breathtaking natural beauty. However, owing to its popularity and protected status as a UNESCO World Heritage Site, visiting Machu Picchu demands considerable planning and preparation. This comprehensive guide aims to provide tourists with an in-depth understanding of how to plan their visit to Machu Picchu, including information on entrance tickets, transportation options, accommodation, recommended itineraries, packing essentials, and practical tips to ensure a smooth and unforgettable journey.

1. Understanding the Significance of Machu Picchu: Before embarking on your expedition, take the time to study about the historical significance of Machu Picchu. Built by the Inca Emperor Pachacuti in the 15th century, this fortress functioned as a royal estate and religious retreat. Abandoned and isolated from the outside world for years, it was unearthed in 1911 by American historian Hiram Bingham. Its enigmatic architecture, complex masonry, and the breathtaking setting of the Andes mountains make it one among the most intriguing archaeological sites in the world.

2. When to Visit Machu Picchu: The optimal time to visit Machu Picchu is during the dry season, which lasts from April to October. During these months, you may expect sunny sky and excellent weather, presenting perfect conditions for exploring the site and walking in the neighbouring environs. The wet season, from November to March, delivers rain and occasionally fog, which may obscure the views. However, Machu Picchu is accessible year-round, and each season provides its particular attraction.

3. Obtaining Machu Picchu entrance Tickets: Securing Machu Picchu entry tickets is the first step in organising your visit. Tickets are limited in number and sell out swiftly, especially during the peak season. Here's how you obtain them:

a. Official Website: Visit the official website of the Ministry of Culture of Peru (https://www.machupicchu.gob.pe/) to purchase your tickets. It's advisable to plan many months in advance, especially if you wish to go during the busy months of June, July, and August.

b. trip companies: If you prefer a guided trip, some credible tour organisations supply Machu Picchu entry tickets as part of their packages.

Ensure that the tour operator is licensed and follows responsible tourism guidelines.

c. Timed entrance: Note that Machu Picchu has a timed entry system, which means you need to choose a set time period for your visit. This helps limit the amount of visitors and safeguard the site's preservation.

d. Huayna Picchu and Machu Picchu Mountain: If you wish to trek either Huayna Picchu or Machu Picchu Mountain, you'll need to buy additional tickets. These hikes give spectacular views of Machu Picchu but require separate advance bookings.

4. Arriving in Aguas Calientes (Machu Picchu Pueblo): Aguas Calientes, also known as Machu Picchu Pueblo, is the gateway town to Machu Picchu. There are numerous means to reach Aguas Calientes:

a. Train: The most typical and easiest method is by taking a train from Cusco or Ollantaytambo to Aguas Calientes. Different train companies offer varied services, including luxury options with panoramic windows.

b. Trekking: For adventurous visitors, trekking the classic Inca Trail or alternative treks like the Salkantay Trek delivers a wonderful excursion through Andean scenery and historic Inca structures. These climbs require prior booking with licenced operators.

c. Bus from Hidroelectrica: For budget visitors, you may reach Hidroelectrica (a hydroelectric station) by bus and then hike or take a train from there to Aguas Calientes.

5. accommodation in Aguas Calientes: Aguas Calientes has several hotel possibilities appealing to all budgets. From peaceful hostels to boutique hotels, there are solutions to meet varied preferences. It's important to arrange your accommodation in advance, especially during busy tourist seasons.

6. Machu Picchu Entrance and Shuttle Bus: On the day of your visit, make sure to be at the right shuttle bus departure site early. Buses run from Aguas Calientes to Machu Picchu commencing at around 5:30 AM. The hike takes roughly 30 minutes, winding up the mountain to the entrance of Machu Picchu.

7. Guided Tours and Local Guides: While exploring Machu Picchu on your own is conceivable, hiring an experienced local guide is strongly encouraged to optimise your experience. Guides provide essential insights into the history, architecture, and cultural importance of the citadel. You may schedule a guide in advance or hire one at the door.

8. dawn and Sunset Visits: Watching the dawn or sunset over Machu Picchu is a spectacular experience. For morning visits, there are few tickets available, so ensure you book early. Watching the sunset above the citadel is also awe-inspiring but often involves purchasing an additional ticket.

9. Recommended Itineraries:

a. Full-Day Visit: A full-day visit to Machu Picchu permits you to explore the principal features of the site, hike to the Sun Gate for a panoramic perspective, and absorb the serene grandeur of this old citadel.

b. Two-Day Visit: For a more relaxed experience, consider spending two days in Machu Picchu. This permits you to explore the site at a leisurely pace, walk to Huayna Picchu or Machu Picchu Mountain, and savour the solitude of the citadel in the early morning and late afternoon.

10. Packing Essentials:

a. Passport: Ensure you carry your passport, because it is needed for entry into Machu Picchu.

b. Comfortable Footwear: Wear robust and comfortable walking shoes, as the terrain at Machu Picchu may be rugged and steep.

c. Water and Snacks: Bring a refillable water bottle and some snacks to keep you energized during your stay.

d. Rain Gear: Even during the dry season, it's recommended to have a rain jacket or poncho, as weather conditions may change abruptly in the Andes.

e. Sun Protection: Don't forget sunscreen, a hat, and sunglasses to protect yourself from the fierce mountain sun.

f. Camera and Binoculars: Capture the gorgeous scenery and wildlife with your camera and binoculars.

g. Sustainable Travel Practices: Carry a reusable water bottle, avoid single-use plastics, and apply the principles of Leave No Trace to ensure responsible travel.

11. height Considerations: Machu Picchu sits at a height of around 2,430 meters (7,970 ft) above sea level. While this is lower than Cusco, it's nevertheless advisable to acclimatize in Cusco or a lower-altitude site before going to reduce altitude-related discomfort.

12. Responsible Tourism and Sustainability: Machu Picchu is a sensitive location, and it's crucial to practise responsible tourism to maintain its natural and cultural history. respect defined trails, refrain from trash, and respect the site's rules and regulations.

Planning Your Visit

Machu Picchu, the famed Inca citadel located in the Andes highlands of Peru, is a bucket-list destination for tourists wishing to witness the grandeur of ancient civilizations and immerse themselves in spectacular natural beauty. However, given to its popularity and protected status as a UNESCO World Heritage Site, visiting Machu Picchu takes meticulous planning and preparation. This comprehensive guide aims to provide tourists with an in-depth understanding of how to plan their visit to Machu Picchu, including information on entrance tickets, transportation options, accommodation, recommended itineraries, packing essentials, and practical tips to ensure a smooth and unforgettable journey.

1. Understanding the Significance of Machu Picchu: Before going on your adventure, take the time to read about the historical significance of Machu Picchu. Built by the Inca Emperor Pachacuti in the 15th century, this castle functioned as a royal estate and religious retreat. Abandoned and concealed from the outer world for generations, it was found in 1911 by American historian Hiram Bingham. Its cryptic design, elaborate masonry, and the stunning background of the Andes mountains make it one of the most interesting archaeological sites in the world.

2. When to Visit Machu Picchu: The optimum time to visit Machu Picchu is during the dry season, which lasts from April to October. During these months, you may anticipate bright sky and nice weather, offering great circumstances for touring the site and trekking in the nearby environs. The rainy season, from

November to March, provides rain and sometimes fog, which may obscure the vistas. However, Machu Picchu is accessible year-round, and each season brings its distinct appeal.

3. **Obtaining Machu Picchu admission Tickets:** Securing Machu Picchu admission tickets is the first step in arranging your journey. Tickets are restricted in quantity and sell out rapidly, particularly during the busy season. Here's how to acquire them:

a. **Official Website:** Visit the official website of the Ministry of Culture of Peru (https://www.machupicchu.gob.pe/) to buy your tickets. It's advised to book several months in advance, particularly if you want to travel during the high months of June, July, and August.

b. trip companies: If you prefer a guided trip, several respectable tour companies provide Machu Picchu admission tickets as part of their packages. Ensure that the tour operator is licensed and follows responsible tourism standards.

c. Timed admission: Note that Machu Picchu has a timed admission system, which means you need to pick a certain time period for your visit. This helps restrict the quantity of visitors and protect the site's preservation.

d. Huayna Picchu and Machu Picchu Mountain: If you intend to walk either Huayna Picchu or Machu Picchu Mountain, you'll need to acquire extra tickets. These climbs provide amazing views of Machu Picchu but need separate previous reservations.

4. Arriving at Aguas Calientes (Machu Picchu Pueblo): Aguas Calientes, also known as Machu Picchu Pueblo, is the gateway town to Machu Picchu. There are various methods to reach Aguas Calientes:

a. Train: The most usual and convenient option is by boarding a train from Cusco or Ollantaytambo to Aguas Calientes. Different train companies provide varying services, including premium alternatives with panoramic windows.

b. Trekking: For adventurous tourists, hiking the classic Inca Trail or alternative treks like the Salkantay Trek gives a wonderful trip through Andean scenery and historic Inca monuments. These hikes need prior booking with approved operators.

c. Bus from Hidroelectrica: For budget tourists, you may reach Hidroelectrica (a hydroelectric station) via bus and then trek or take a train from there to Aguas Calientes.

5. lodging in Aguas Calientes: Aguas Calientes provides numerous lodging alternatives appealing to all budgets. From quiet hostels to boutique hotels, there are alternatives to suit diverse interests. It's advisable to reserve your accommodation in advance, particularly during busy tourist seasons.

6. Machu Picchu Entrance and Shuttle Bus: On the day of your visit, be sure to arrive at the appropriate shuttle bus departure location early. Buses go from Aguas Calientes to Machu Picchu beginning at roughly 5:30 AM. The trek takes around 30 minutes, meandering up the mountain to the entrance to Machu Picchu.

7. Guided Tours and Local Guides: While seeing Machu Picchu on your own is doable, hiring an experienced local guide is highly advised to improve your experience. Guides give significant insights into the history, architecture, and cultural relevance of the citadel. You may arrange a guide in advance or hire one at the entry.

8. Sunrise and Sunset Visits: Watching the sunrise or sunset above Machu Picchu is a beautiful experience. For morning visits, there are limited tickets available, so ensure you reserve early. Watching the sunset over the citadel is likewise awe-inspiring but typically needs obtaining an extra ticket.

9. Recommended Itineraries:

a. Full-Day Visit: A full-day visit to Machu Picchu enables you to see the major points of the site, trek to the Sun Gate for a panoramic perspective, and appreciate the tranquil majesty of this ancient fortress.

b. **Two-Day Visit:** For a more leisurely experience, try spending two days at Machu Picchu. This enables you to explore the site at a leisurely pace, trek to Huayna Picchu or Machu Picchu Mountain, and appreciate the quiet of the citadel in the early morning and late afternoon.

10. Packing Essentials:

a. **Passport:** Ensure you bring your passport, since it is essential for admittance into Machu Picchu.

b. **Comfortable Footwear:** Wear strong and comfortable walking shoes, since the terrain at Machu Picchu can be rough and steep.

c. **Water and Snacks:** Bring a refillable water bottle and some snacks to keep you energized throughout your stay.

d. Rain Gear: Even during the dry season, it's wise to take a rain jacket or poncho, since weather conditions may change suddenly in the Andes.

e. Sun Protection: Don't forget sunscreen, a hat, and sunglasses to protect yourself from the powerful mountain sun.

f. Camera and Binoculars: Capture the stunning landscape and animals with your camera and binoculars.

g. Sustainable Travel Practices: Carry a reusable water bottle, avoid single-use plastics, and practise the principles of Leave No Trace to guarantee responsible travel.

11. height Considerations: Machu Picchu is at a height of roughly 2,430 meters (7,970 feet) above sea level. While this is lower than Cusco, it's still suggested to acclimatize at

Cusco or a lower-altitude place before going to minimise altitude-related discomfort.

12. Responsible Tourism and Sustainability: Machu Picchu is a vulnerable place, and it's vital to conduct responsible tourism to conserve its natural and cultural legacy. Follow established paths, abstain from littering, and follow the site's laws and regulations.

How to Get to Machu Picchu

Machu Picchu, the ancient Incan fortress located high in the Andes Mountains of Peru, is one of the most famous and sought-after places in the world. Accessing this awe-inspiring ancient treasure needs meticulous preparation, since the trek entails various transit choices and ticket reservations. This detailed guide seeks to aid travellers in finding their way to Machu Picchu while assuring a memorable and delightful trip.

I. Choose Your Route:

1. Classic Inca path: A four-day walk travelling through breathtaking scenery and Inca sites, this path provides a physically difficult yet rewarding adventure. Permits are necessary and should be acquired well in advance.

2. Inca trek Alternatives: If the traditional trek is already booked, explore alternate routes like the Salkantay Trek or the Lares Trek, providing various landscapes and cultural experiences.

3. Train from Cusco: Opt for a more pleasant and shorter travel by taking a picturesque train ride from Cusco to Aguas Calientes, the town closest to Machu Picchu.

II. Arriving in Cusco:

1. Flights to Cusco: Most foreign travellers land in Lima, Peru's capital, and then take a domestic flight to Cusco, the gateway city to Machu Picchu.

2. Altitude Adjustment: Cusco resides at a high altitude, so allow a day or two to acclimatize before commencing any excursions or tours.

III. Acquiring Machu Picchu Entrance Tickets:

1. Official Website: Purchase admission tickets directly from the official Machu Picchu website or via approved agents.

2. Availability and Limits: Tickets have limited availability each day, particularly for the Inca Trail, so book well in advance, especially during high seasons.

IV. Organized Tours vs. Independent Travel:

1. Organized Tours: Joining a guided trip gives convenience and competence, but be sure you select reliable providers.

2. Independent Travel: For greater freedom, organise your vacation independently, booking transportation, lodgings, and tickets on your own.

V. Reaching Aguas Calientes:

1. Train Options: Choose between several train services, such as Expedition, Vistadome, and the premium Belmond Hiram Bingham, each giving differing degrees of comfort and facilities.

2. Bus from Aguas Calientes: From Aguas Calientes, take a short yet gorgeous bus trip up to the entrance of Machu Picchu.

VI. Exploring Machu Picchu:

1. Guided Tours: Consider hiring a local guide at the entrance to improve your experience and obtain insights into the historical importance of the place.

2. Best Time to Visit: Arrive early in the morning or late in the afternoon to avoid crowds and enjoy the mysterious ambience.

VII. Huayna Picchu and Machu Picchu Mountain:

1. Optional Hikes: If you have the energy and necessary permissions, try trekking Huayna Picchu or Machu Picchu Mountain for breathtaking panoramic vistas.

VIII. Return to Cusco:

1. Train Back to Cusco: Board the train from Aguas Calientes back to Cusco to complete your Machu Picchu tour.

Guided Tours vs. Independent Visits

Machu Picchu, the ancient Incan fortress situated high in the Andes of Peru, is a

UNESCO World Heritage Site and one of the New Seven Wonders of the World. For travellers, it gives a once-in-a-lifetime chance to experience a fascinating combination of history, culture, and stunning beauty. When arranging a visit to Machu Picchu, tourists typically face the challenge of selecting between guided tours and individual trips. Each choice has its benefits, and recognising their pros and downsides may dramatically effect your experience at this magnificent place.

Section 1: The Benefits of Guided Tours

Expert Knowledge: Guided tours to Machu Picchu are guided by professional guides who are well-versed in the history, architecture, and importance of the monument. They give significant insights and tales, bringing the historic city to life and improving tourists' knowledge and enjoyment of its cultural legacy. Guides also highlight important elements that can be ignored during an autonomous visit, enabling guests establish a stronger connection to this historical masterpiece.

scheduled Itinerary: One of the primary benefits of guided excursions is their scheduled itinerary. These trips follow preset pathways and timetables, delivering travellers to major sights inside Machu Picchu. This systematic method guarantees that tourists do not miss out on crucial features and essential historical information. Additionally, guides can effectively browse the site, maximizing the time spent at each spot and enhancing the overall touring experience.

Group Dynamics: Traveling as a group on a guided trip may generate a sense of camaraderie among members. Meeting other visitors from diverse origins and cultures offers a common experience, allowing for intriguing talks and the possibility to make new friends.

For single travelers or those wanting a more social experience, guided tours may provide a more engaging and engaged encounter.

Logistics and Planning: Booking a guided trip typically relieves guests of the logistical constraints involved with visiting Machu Picchu solo. Tour providers organise transportation to and from the destination, handle admittance fees and permits, and manage other practical parts of the excursion. This ease enables visitors to concentrate exclusively on absorbing the site's beauty and history without bothering about detailed preparation.

Section 2: The Advantages of Independent Visits

Flexibility: Independent trips allow the opportunity to explore Machu Picchu at your own leisure. Travelers may spend longer time at their favourite sites, engage in particular hobbies, and immerse themselves in the serene environment of the site. Unlike guided tours, where time limitations may determine the duration of stay at each sight, independent tourists may spend as much time as they wish to completely absorb the enthralling surroundings.

Photography Opportunities: Machu Picchu's magnificent panoramas and renowned monuments make it a heaven for photographers. Independent guests have the benefit of capturing individual moments without being pressured. Photographers might patiently wait for the optimum lighting conditions or pick off-peak hours to avoid crowds, resulting in breathtaking and distinctive photographs that express their personal relationship to the location.

single Adventure: For single travelers seeking solitude and self-reflection, autonomous trips provide an unrivalled experience. The calm environment of Machu Picchu helps people to interact with the monument on a more intimate level, promoting reflection and a profound understanding of the site's historical importance. Solo travelers have the option to customise their vacation according to their tastes and experience an uninterrupted and soul-stirring adventure.

Cost-Effectiveness: Independent travelers have the ability to save money on their Machu Picchu adventure. By controlling their spending prudently, picking for budget-friendly hotel, transportation, and food alternatives, they can modify the vacation to match their budgetary limits. Moreover, independent tourists have the freedom to pick affordable admission tickets and explore the site without spending extra guide expenses.

Section 3: Considerations for Guided Tours

Group Size: The size of the tour group may considerably effect the guided tour experience. Smaller groups often give a more intimate and customised interaction with the guide, giving for more opportunity to ask questions and join in conversations. On the other side, bigger groups may lead to congestion in popular sites, reducing the quality of the experience for some participants.

Tour Operator Reputation: Selecting a respected tour operator is vital for a successful guided tour experience. Researching and reading reviews about various tour companies may help ensure that travellers pick operators with experienced guides, responsible methods, and great customer feedback. A well-chosen tour operator may increase the experience of the trip by delivering exceptional services and important insights.

Time Limitations: Guided tours frequently adhere to particular time restrictions to suit the schedules of various participants. This time constraint may restrict the amount of time spent at each sight or attraction, leaving some tourists seeking more unhurried exploration. For people with a significant interest in some areas of Machu Picchu, such as photography or architectural complexities, guided excursions may not give enough time for in-depth inspection.

Section 4: Considerations for Independent Visits

Research and organising: Independent travelers must devote time and effort in studying and organising their Machu Picchu journey. Understanding the site's history, importance, and logistical elements is vital to making a pleasant voyage. Researching alternative hiking routes, lodgings, tickets choices, and local rules can help guests to make educated selections and optimise their stay at the destination.

Language Barrier: Peru's official language is Spanish, and although English is often spoken in tourist regions, language hurdles may still be an issue for independent travelers, especially in less touristic locales. Learning some basic Spanish words or carrying a translation tool may assist bridge the communication gap and enhance contact with locals.

Navigation: Exploring Machu Picchu solo demands a solid sense of direction and navigation abilities. The site's size may be intimidating, and without a guide, travellers may struggle to discover particular places of interest or navigate around the labyrinthine stone buildings. However, with proper planning, utilising maps, and understanding the layout beforehand, independent visitors may comfortably tour the site on their own terms.

Hiking the Inca Trail

The Inca Trail, a fabled ancient trail in Peru, is one of the world's most known trekking paths. Spanning around 26 miles (42 kilometers) across the Andes Mountains, this trek brings visitors to the breathtaking remains of Machu Picchu, a renowned Incan citadel and UNESCO World Heritage Site. This thorough book is aimed to aid travellers in organising an outstanding trekking trip on the Inca Trail. From knowing its historical importance to preparing for the trek, we'll examine every facet of this epic expedition.

Section 1: The Historical and Cultural Significance of the Inca Trail

The Inca Trail possesses great historical and cultural importance as a hallowed pilgrimage path for the Incan Empire. In ancient times, it functioned as a significant gateway for religious rites and spiritual trips to the cherished sanctuary of Machu Picchu. This historical link makes the route an extraordinary experience, enabling hikers to follow in the footsteps of the Inca civilisation and develop a better respect for their creativity and love for environment.

Along the walk, trekkers meet spectacular archaeological monuments, affording an insight into the architectural marvels of the Incas. Wiñay Wayna, an exquisite terraced site, exhibits the agricultural skill of the Incas, while Phuyupatamarca, known as the "Town Above the Clouds," gives stunning views of the surrounding valleys and mountains. These well-preserved ruins serve as a testimony to the Inca civilization's sophisticated engineering capabilities and urban design.

Section 2: Planning Your Inca Trail Adventure

To begin on this expedition, travellers must get permissions, since the Inca Trail is a heavily controlled path. Due to its popularity and to conserve its natural beauty, the Peruvian government limited the number of tourists each day, making early reservations important. Tourists may get permits directly from the Peruvian Ministry of Culture or via certified tour companies, and it is advised to book well in advance, particularly during the peak trekking season.

The optimal time to trek the Inca Trail is during the dry season, from May to September. During these months, rainfall is negligible, and the weather is often clear, affording stunning vistas and suitable trekking conditions.

However, this season corresponds with increasing demand, so acquiring permits and reserving reservations early is vital.

Since individual trekking is not authorised on the Inca Trail, travellers must arrange a certified tour operator to join them on the route. Choosing a reliable and skilled operator assures a well-organized and safe tour. These trip packages normally include transportation, lunches, camping equipment, and expert guides, making the trek hassle-free and enriching.

Section 3: Preparing for the Hike

The Inca Trail is considered a moderate to tough trek, requiring hikers to be in excellent physical shape. Preparing with regular exercise and cardiovascular fitness is vital to completely enjoy the trip and decrease the danger of altitude-related health complications.

Due to the trail's high height, acclimation is necessary to prevent altitude sickness. Spending a few days in Cusco or other high-altitude regions before commencing the trip helps the body acclimatise to the lower oxygen levels, minimising the chance of pain and sickness throughout the journey.

A detailed packing list is vital for a pleasant and safe travel. Essential supplies include adequate clothes for varied weather situations, robust and well-broken-in hiking boots, camping gear, a first-aid kit, and personal stuff. Packing light is necessary, since porters and mules carry the bulk of the camping equipment and supplies.

Section 4: The Inca Trail Experience

The Inca Trail normally runs four days and three nights, spanning varied terrains and elevations. The day-by-day schedule is meticulously organised to deliver a balanced and delightful hiking experience, bringing hikers through varied environments, from high mountain passes to beautiful cloud forests.

One of the highlights of the path is reaching the Sun Gate, or Intipunku, on the last day of the journey. From this vantage point, travellers got their first view of Machu Picchu at daybreak. The overpowering feelings of reaching this legendary site make the long trek all the more gratifying.

Throughout the walk, hikers are immersed in the spectacular Andean landscapes, travelling through breathtaking vistas and distinct ecological zones. The rich flora and animals found along the path provide wonderful opportunity for nature enthusiasts and wildlife lovers.

Camping is a vital element of the Inca Trail experience. Tour operators offer pleasant campsites and food, creating a feeling of camaraderie among hikers as they exchange tales and experiences over the campfire.

Section 5: Respecting Nature and Cultural Heritage

Responsible tourism is crucial to protect the integrity of the Inca Trail and its surrounding ecosystem. Following standards imposed by park officials, such as "Leave No Trace" principles, ensures that hikers limit their influence on the delicate ecological and cultural monuments. Refraining from trash, respecting animals, and sticking on authorised trails are vital in sustaining the trail's unspoiled beauty.

As the path goes through multiple local towns, connecting with people and learning about their customs and way of life improves the hiking experience. Being courteous and attentive to their practises and beliefs encourages cultural interchange and mutual understanding, generating a good influence on both visitors and residents.

Section 6: Arriving at Machu Picchu

The last day of the walk leads to the Sun Gate, where tourists gain their first view of Machu Picchu at daybreak. This moment is filled with amazement and a feeling of success, as hikers grasp the immensity of their trek and the satisfaction of reaching this legendary location.

Upon descending to Machu Picchu, trekkers start on a guided tour of the ancient site. A skilled guide goes into its history, architecture, and riddles, unveiling the intriguing narrative of the old fortress. The mix of physical hardship and intellectual growth makes this contact with Machu Picchu a very unique experience.

Chapter 6: Surrounding Archaeological Sites

Nestled in the midst of the Andes mountains, the city of Cusco, Peru, has a treasure trove of archaeological monuments that take tourists back in time to the glory days of the Inca civilisation. Surrounded by a myriad of historic landmarks, Cusco remains as a living witness to the inventiveness, craftsmanship, and spiritual importance of the once-mighty Inca Empire. In this detailed guide, we welcome travellers to go on a captivating trip to explore the surrounding ancient sites in Cusco and uncover the mysteries that lay beneath their stone walls.

1. Sacsayhuaman:

Perched high above Cusco, the majestic castle of Sacsayhuaman boasts spectacular panoramic views of the city below. Constructed from enormous limestone stones skillfully connected without the use of cement, Sacsayhuaman exhibits the incredible technical skills of the Inca civilization. Its cryptic function, considered to be a religious, administrative, or defensive site, continues to interest scholars and tourists alike.

2. Machu Picchu:

No trip of Cusco's ancient sites would be complete without a visit to the famed Machu Picchu. Often referred to as the "Lost City of the Incas," this UNESCO World Heritage site is one of the most well-preserved archaeological marvels in the world. Hidden between lush green mountains and foggy clouds, Machu Picchu exhibits the superior urban planning and astronomical knowledge held by the Inca culture. Tourists may go on the legendary Inca Trail or choose for a picturesque train excursion to reach this awe-inspiring location.

3. Pisac:

Situated in the Sacred Valley of the Incas, the historic site of Pisac enchants tourists with its spectacular terraces, ancient temples, and complicated agricultural systems. The Intihuatana, a ceremonial stone related with astronomical observations, is a focal point of spiritual importance at Pisac. Additionally, the neighbouring Pisac Market allows guests a chance to immerse themselves in the colourful local culture and acquire unique handcrafted items.

4. Moray:

Moray is a fascinating location marked by a sequence of circular terraces descending into the soil. It is thought to have acted as an agricultural laboratory where the Inca experimented with different crops, taking use of microclimates inside the concentric circles. The accuracy of the terraces' construction and the site's strategic position make Moray a tribute to the Incas' expertise in exploiting the land's resources.

5. Ollantaytambo:

The stronghold of Ollantaytambo is a monument to the Inca's excellent military architecture and strategic city planning. It functioned as a fortress and a ceremonial center, showcasing huge stone blocks and beautiful stone-carved fountains. Ollantaytambo is also a starting point for many people travelling to Machu Picchu via the Inca Trail.

6. Choquequirao:

Known as the "Sister City of Machu Picchu," Choquequirao remains largely unknown, presenting intrepid tourists with a feeling of adventure as they explore its extensive terraces, temples, and residential sections. The trip to Choquequirao is arduous but rewards tourists with a feeling of exclusivity and a deep connection to the ancient past.

7. Tipon:

The archaeological site at Tipon displays the Inca's excellent grasp of hydraulic engineering. With its remarkable irrigation channels and water terraces, Tipon functioned as a ceremonial center and an agricultural laboratory, displaying the Incas' knowledge of sustainable farming methods.

Choquequirao

Nestled deep among the Andean highlands of Cusco, Peru, sits the intriguing archaeological site of Choquequirao. Often referred to as the

"Sister City of Machu Picchu," Choquequirao remains a hidden treasure, enticing daring travellers with its secluded setting, well-preserved ruins, and rich historical importance. In this detailed book, we welcome tourists to go on a fascinating trip to uncover the secrets of Choquequirao, learn about its ancient history, and immerse themselves in the mesmerising beauty of this lesser-known Inca masterpiece.

1. Historical Background:

Choquequirao owes its origins back to the Inca civilisation, which thrived throughout the 15th and 16th centuries. The site is considered to have been an important religious, administrative, and agricultural hub, ideally positioned to supervise and link different sections of the enormous Inca Empire. The actual function of Choquequirao remains a source of discussion among historians, contributing to its attraction as a location of mysterious importance.

2. The Meaning of Choquequirao:

The name "Choquequirao" is derived from two Quechua words: "choque," meaning "golden," and "quirao," meaning "cradle" or "cradle of gold." The name symbolises the grandeur and spiritual importance connected with the location, potentially hinting at the wealth or holiness it formerly contained. Despite its interesting name, Choquequirao remains a relatively undiscovered monument compared to its iconic sibling, Machu Picchu.

3. Access and Location:

Choquequirao's isolated location and hard access have contributed to its preservation and lesser-known status. Situated at a height of around 3,050 meters (10,000 feet) above sea level, the location may be accessed by a multi-day walk or by renting horses or mules to carry supplies. The route to Choquequirao is an adventure in itself, as tourists pass through steep terrain, thick woods, and traversing deep river valleys.

4. The Choquequirao Trek:

The hike to Choquequirao is an excursion for the intrepid and environment aficionados. It normally takes around four to five days, depending on the route selected and individual hiking speed. Unlike the strictly controlled Inca Trail to Machu Picchu, the Choquequirao trip gives a feeling of exclusivity and privacy, enabling guests to connect profoundly with the stunning vistas and immerse themselves in the calm of the Andean environment.

5. Archaeological Highlights:

Choquequirao's archaeological complex sprawls across an area of around 1,800 hectares (4,447 acres), showcasing a plethora of well-preserved buildings that give insights into the Inca way of life. The primary topics of interest include:

- **Main Plaza:** An large open area surrounded by ceremonial buildings, exhibiting the Incas' architectural brilliance and their respect for heavenly bodies and the natural environment.

- **Llamas Terraces:** A series of terraces resembling the back of a llama, displaying the Inca's creative farming practises to increase food production in the tough hilly environment.

- **Temples and Residential Areas:** Several temples and residential constructions, such as the Temple of the Sun and the House of the Priest, give insights into the religious and everyday life of the ancient people of Choquequirao.

- **Usnu:** A ceremonial platform where rites and ceremonies were held, frequently tied to astronomical observations and agricultural events, demonstrating the Incas' spiritual connection to the universe.

6. The Three Levels of Choquequirao:

Choquequirao is separated into three levels, each having a specific purpose:

- **Hanan:** The higher level, devoted to religious and ceremonial activities, generally reserved for the aristocracy and high priests.

- **Urin:** The middle level, mostly consisting of agricultural terraces, used to raise a range of crops to maintain the site's inhabitants.

- **Hurin:** The lowest level, typified by residential and administrative buildings, symbolising the everyday lives of the common people and employees.

7. Significance and Discovery:

While Machu Picchu draws millions of tourists each, Choquequirao remains a hidden gem, waiting to be thoroughly explored and appreciated. The place received worldwide notice in the 18th century when the Spanish explorer Juan Arias Diaz stumbled across it during his investigations of the area. However, important archaeological study and preservation initiatives started much later in the 20th century, spearheaded by notable scientists and organisations.

8. Preservation and Conservation:

As a UNESCO World history candidate, Choquequirao is subject to severe preservation and conservation efforts to conserve its fragile buildings and unique history. Responsible tourist practices are crucial, with visitors urged to follow criteria put out by local authorities to limit the damage on the environment and archaeological sites.

9. The Future of Choquequirao:

With increased interest from visitors and academics, Choquequirao has the potential to become a significant archaeological and cultural site in Cusco. However, finding a balance between expanding tourists and conserving the site's originality remains a struggle. Sustainable development, community engagement, and ethical tourist practices are vital in protecting Choquequirao for future generations to treasure.

10. Practical Tips for Travelers:

a. **Physical Fitness:** The Choquequirao trip is extremely difficult, and tourists are urged to be in excellent condition before beginning on the adventure. Regular exercise and acclimation in Cusco are vital prerequisites.

b. **Weather:** The climate in the Andes may be unpredictable, with temperature changes throughout the day. Proper attire, especially layers and rain gear, is necessary.

c. **Permits:** As Choquequirao tries to conserve its pristine state, restricted daily admission permits are provided. It is essential to obtain permits in advance to reserve a position.

d. **Guided Tours:** Hiring a skilled guide would improve the experience by offering historical context and assuring a safe walk.

e. Camping: Camping facilities are provided on the walk, however it is important to arrange in advance.

Tipon

Nestled within the breathtaking scenery of the Sacred Valley of the Incas, Tipon stands as a tribute to the technical brilliance and agricultural skill of the Inca civilisation. Often overlooked by its more renowned rivals, such as Machu Picchu and Ollantaytambo, this archaeological masterpiece provides a riveting experience for interested travellers looking to investigate the inventiveness of the past. In this detailed guide, we dig into the delights of Tipon, giving historical background, architectural importance, practical recommendations, and the finest methods to immerse oneself in this hidden treasure of Cusco.

1. Historical Background:

Tipon, also known as "Water Temple," was erected during the time of the eighth Inca emperor, Pachacuti Inca Yupanqui, in the 15th century. This complex structure operated as a key agricultural and religious center, demonstrating the Incas' extensive mastery of hydraulic engineering. Situated at the foot of the Pachatusan mountain, Tipon's architecture centred on water management, which played a critical role in supporting the agricultural terraces and guaranteeing a stable water supply to the neighbouring farmlands.

2. Location and Access:

Tipon is ideally situated roughly 24 kilometers (15 miles) southeast of Cusco, making it readily accessible for day visits from the capital. Travelers may reach Tipon via vehicle, bus, or guided trips. The drive from Cusco to

Tipon provides stunning vistas of the Andean scenery, enabling tourists to immerse themselves in the natural splendour of the area.

3. Architectural Marvels:

The principal interest of Tipon resides in its innovative irrigation system, which is a magnificent marvel of Inca engineering. A network of stone channels, fountains, and terraces are integrated to control and transport water from neighbouring springs. The accuracy and artistry of the masonry are awe-inspiring, with each stone precisely carved and put together without the use of mortar. The genius of the water system is obvious when tourists explore the well-preserved terraces and canals that continue to work to this day.

4. The Water Features:

As the "Water Temple," Tipon contains an assortment of intriguing water elements that illustrate the Inca's devotion for this life-giving resource. The most noticeable water feature is the spectacular tiered water garden, where the cascading channels create a fascinating display. The fountains, known as "chachacomas," were supposed to reflect the perpetual flow of life, with water signifying cleanliness and fertility in Inca mythology. The calming sound of running water against the background of the Andean mountains adds to the serenity and mysticism of the setting.

5. Agricultural Terraces:

Beyond its hydraulic technical wonders, Tipon's agricultural terraces represent the Incas' strong relationship with nature and their sustainable farming techniques. The terraces were meticulously planned to use the mountain's microclimates, allowing for the production of a varied variety of crops. The site's elevation differences produce unique growth conditions for numerous agricultural items, including as maize, potatoes, and quinoa, which remain crucial to the region's subsistence agriculture.

6. Spiritual and Religious Significance:

Apart from its agricultural and technical value, Tipon also carries sacred relevance for the Incas. The strategic placement and layout of the site are thought to correlate with astronomical occurrences and celestial alignments, relating it to their spiritual beliefs and ceremonies. Many hypotheses imply that Tipon may have acted as a venue for religious events and astronomical studies, further enhancing its magical charm.

7. Exploring Tipon:

Visiting Tipon provides a wonderful experience through Inca history and natural beauty. As you explore the terraces, fountains, and channels, take a minute to admire the balance between human creativity and the surrounding nature. A leisurely stroll through the terraced gardens and along the water channels gives a chance to connect with the Inca's great reverence for water and their sustainable farming techniques.

8. Practical Tips for Travelers:

a. Visiting Hours: Tipon is open everyday from dawn to late afternoon. It is suggested to come early to avoid crowds and make the most of your experience.

b. Footwear: Comfortable walking shoes are needed, as the site entails navigating rough terrain.

c. Sun Protection: The high-altitude Andean sun may be fierce, so don't forget sunscreen, a hat, and sunglasses.

d. Hydration: Bring an extra quantity of water to remain hydrated during your vacation, particularly during sunny days.

a. Tour Guide: Hiring a competent tour guide will boost your understanding of Tipon's historical and cultural significance.

9. Combining Tipon with Other Attractions:

Tipon's closeness to other prominent Inca ruins gives a chance for travellers to arrange a thorough itinerary. Consider combining your visit to Tipon with adjacent sights like as Pikillacta, a historic pre-Inca settlement, and Andahuaylillas, renowned as the "Sistine Chapel of the Andes." This manner, you may experience a varied variety of ancient treasures in a single day.

Piquillacta

Nestled in the mountains of the Cusco area in Peru, Piquillacta remains as a spectacular witness to the technical brilliance and cultural importance of the ancient Wari civilisation. This lesser-known ancient site, situated only 30 kilometers southeast of Cusco, provides an incredible voyage back in time for history aficionados and inquisitive tourists alike. In this detailed guide, we will dig into the enthralling history, beautiful architecture, and practical travel suggestions that make Piquillacta a must-visit site for travellers looking to unravel the secrets of Peru's rich past.

I. Historical Background:

Piquillacta, which means "Flea Town" in the Quechua language, was an important administrative and ceremonial center erected by the Wari civilisation approximately 550 AD. The Wari, a pre-Inca culture, prospered in the area between 500 and 1000 AD, and Piquillacta was one of their most major urban centres. As an important outpost in their enormous empire, the location played a critical role in promoting commerce, government, and religious activities.

II. Architecture and Layout:

Spanning over 50 hectares, Piquillacta features a remarkable urban architecture typified by well-organized streets, beautifully aligned structures, and elaborate water management systems. The arrangement demonstrates the Wari's profound grasp of urban planning and architectural engineering.

1. The Citadel: The great citadel of Piquillacta has many multi-story constructions made from stone and adobe. Visitors may experience the distinctive architectural style of the Wari, which is different from that of the subsequent Inca culture. The walls are finely built, with perfectly cut stones, and the buildings give an insight into the everyday life of the Wari people.

2. Residential Quarters: Beyond the citadel, visitors will uncover a number of residential quarters, proof of a bustling community that previously occupied the site. The Wari were renowned for their urban lifestyle, and their buildings give insight into their home routines and social organization.

3. Temples & Religious Complexes: Piquillacta contains various temples and religious areas where the Wari conducted their spiritual beliefs. The architectural complexity and symbolic significance of these monuments reflect the religious value of the place within the Wari civilisation.

III. Cultural Significance:

Piquillacta functioned as a crucial connection in the massive Wari road network that linked different sections of the empire. As an administrative hub, it played a major role in coordinating economic operations, managing far-flung territory, and enabling communication between various regions. Furthermore, the site's strategic placement at the intersection of multiple trade routes led to its significance in the Wari culture.

IV. Tips for Tourists:

1. Getting There: Piquillacta is readily accessible from Cusco by several forms of transportation. Travelers may select for guided excursions, private taxis, or rental automobiles to reach the location conveniently. The travel takes around one hour, and the picturesque drive gives spectacular views of the Andean countryside.

2. Ideal Time to Visit: The greatest time to explore Piquillacta is during the dry season, from April to October. During these months, the weather is typically good, and rain is less likely to disturb your stay. However, be prepared for lower temperatures, particularly in the nights, since the location is located at a height of roughly 3,400 meters above sea level.

3. Guided Tours: To properly appreciate the historical importance and architectural splendour of Piquillacta, consider hiring a knowledgable local guide. Expert guides may give vital insights, interesting anecdotes, and historical background that improve the whole experience.

4. Respect the Site: As with any archaeological site, it is crucial to respect Piquillacta's legacy and help maintain its integrity for future generations. Avoid touching or climbing on the old buildings, and be cautious of any rules put out by the local authorities.

5. Pack Essentials: Bring comfortable walking shoes, sun protection (hats, sunscreen), a refillable water bottle, and a camera to record the stunning landscape and architectural treasures.

Chapter 7: Cultural Experiences

Cusco, the ancient capital of the Inca Empire, maintains a compelling fascination for tourists looking to immerse themselves in the vivid tapestry of Peruvian culture. Nestled in the magnificent Andes Mountains, this lovely city provides a multitude of cultural events that exhibit its historic origins, colonial influences, and current customs. In this complete guide, we will explore the varied spectrum of cultural interactions that await travellers in Cusco, from discovering ancient archaeological sites and colourful marketplaces to partaking in traditional celebrations and eating wonderful Peruvian food.

I. Historical and Archaeological Treasures:

1. Sacsayhuaman: A UNESCO World Heritage site, Sacsayhuaman is an awe-inspiring Inca castle situated just outside Cusco. Marvel at the gigantic stone walls that fit together without the need of mortar, a monument to the genius of Inca engineering. Visit during the Inti Raymi festival in June to experience an extraordinary recreation of an old Inca celebration.

2. **Qorikancha:** Once the most prominent temple of the Inca Empire, Qorikancha, or the Temple of the Sun, exhibits the blending of Inca architecture with Spanish colonial elements. Observe the masterfully constructed masonry and the confluence of two unique civilizations in this amazing historical place.

3. **Tambomachay, Puka Pukara, and Q'enqo:** These lesser-known archaeological sites give insight into the Inca's complex water management, military operations, and religious rituals. Explore the exquisite stone sculptures

and natural rock formations that once played key roles in the Inca civilisation.

II. Vibrant Markets and Handicrafts:

1. San Pedro Market: Located in the centre of Cusco, the busy San Pedro Market gives a genuine peek into the Peruvian way of life. Engage your senses as you travel through the maze of vendors selling fresh vegetables, traditional Andean meals, handmade crafts, and artisanal products.

2. Pisac Market: Venture to the picturesque village of Pisac, where a colourful market comes alive every Sunday. Shop for elaborately woven textiles, bright pottery, and unusual gifts while enjoying the lovely location surrounded by the Andean mountains.

3. Chinchero Textile Center: Visit the Chinchero Textile Center, where local weavers showcase the craft of traditional textile-making. Learn about the natural dyes and old procedures that have been handed down through centuries, producing exquisite patterns and motifs.

III. Festivals and Celebrations:

1. Inti Raymi: Experience the largest event of the Inca Empire, Inti Raymi, around the winter solstice on June 24th. Witness a fascinating theatrical performance at Sacsayhuaman, honouring the old Inca Sun God with bright costumes, music, and dancing.

2. Qoyllur Rit'i: Held in May or June, Qoyllur Rit'i is a unique combination of traditional Andean beliefs and Catholic traditions. Join hundreds of pilgrims as they make their journey to the Sinakara Sanctuary, high in the Andes, for a spiritual and cultural feast.

3. Corpus Christi: Cusco's most major religious celebration, Corpus Christi, happens 60 days after Easter Sunday. Watch as streets come alive with religious processions, music, and beautiful displays highlighting Cusco's religious devotion.

IV. Gastronomic Delights:

1. Try Traditional Peruvian Dishes: Indulge in exquisite Peruvian food, famed for its unique flavors and utilisation of indigenous ingredients. Savor Ceviche, Anticuchos (grilled skewers), Lomo Saltado (stir-fried beef), and Aji de Gallina (chicken in chili cream sauce) at local diners and restaurants.

2. Pachamanca: Experience the traditional cooking process of Pachamanca, where food is made underground using hot stones. This classic Andean feast includes pork, potatoes, maize, and other components, providing a flavorsome gastronomic experience.

V. Immersive Cultural Workshops:

1. Andean Music and Dance: Participate in courses that expose you to Andean musical instruments, such as the pan flute and charango. Learn classic dances like the Marinera and Huayno, and appreciate the rhythm and beauty of Peruvian folk culture.

2. Cooking lessons: Enroll in cooking lessons to learn how to produce genuine Peruvian foods from skilled chefs. Discover the techniques of mixing local ingredients to produce distinct tastes that distinguish Peruvian cooking.

Traditional Festivals

Cusco, nestled in the heart of the Peruvian Andes, is a city immersed in rich cultural history and old customs. Among its numerous attractions, the traditional festivals of Cusco occupy a particular position, providing a look into the vivid traditions, colorful festivities, and deep-rooted history of this wonderful area. As a visitor visiting Cusco, immersing oneself in these indigenous celebrations will certainly be a wonderful experience.

1. Introducing Cusco and Its Festivals

Cusco, originally the capital of the Inca Empire, is now a UNESCO World Heritage site noted for its well-preserved Inca monuments, Spanish colonial architecture, and vibrant marketplaces. However, it is during the different festivals hosted throughout the year that the city really comes alive with intensity and enthusiasm. These celebrations are a mix of pre-Columbian Andean customs and Catholic ceremonies introduced by the Spanish conquistadors, resulting in a unique blend of spirituality, folklore, and fun.

2. Inti Raymi - The Festival of the Sun

Perhaps the most renowned and prominent celebration in Cusco is Inti Raymi, commonly known as the celebration of the Sun. Celebrated annually on June 24th, the winter solstice in the Southern Hemisphere, Inti Raymi pays respect to the Inca sun deity, Inti. The celebrations start at the old castle of Sacsayhuaman, where a recreation of the ancient rite takes place. Dressed in traditional colorful clothes, dancers and actors replicate ancient rites, including gifts to the sun and soil.

3. Qoyllur Rit'i - The Star Snow Festival

Another unique event in Cusco is Qoyllur Rit'i, celebrated in the Sinakara Valley around May or June. This unusual event blends Andean beliefs with Christian components, and it is dedicated to the Lord of Qoyllur Rit'i, who is supposed to safeguard the region's animals and crops. Thousands of pilgrims, including indigenous groups from the surrounding highlands, make their way to the Sinakara Valley, producing a stunning scene of colorful tents and processions.

4. Virgen del Carmen - The Mamacha Carmen Festival

In July, the little Andean community of Paucartambo, situated a few hours from Cusco, holds the Virgen del Carmen festival. This religious feast, also known as the Mamacha Carmen Festival, commemorates the patron saint of Paucartambo. Dancers wrapped in extravagant costumes go to the streets, performing ancient dances with tremendous excitement and intensity. The festival's culmination is a symbolic combat between the Christians and the Incas, reflecting the historical clash of civilizations.

5. Corpus Christi - The Feast of the Body of Christ

One of the most famous religious festivals in Cusco is the Corpus Christi feast, occurring 60 days following Easter Sunday. This Catholic event shows an astounding exhibition of holy art, including elaborate silver sculptures and precious relics. The major attraction of the celebration is the great procession of the venerated figure of Christ, which is carried through the streets of Cusco amid traditional music and dancing.

6. Pachamama - The Mother Earth Festival
Deeply steeped in Andean theology, the Pachamama event pays respect to Mother Earth, a venerated divinity in the Andean pantheon. Held in August, this event features rituals of thanksgiving and sacrifices to Pachamama for a good crop and protection against natural calamities. Local communities meet to execute rites, such as burying gifts of food, coca leaves, and other symbolic objects in the ground as a manner of pleasing the soil.

7. Independence Day Celebrations

On July 28th and 29th, Cusco honours Peru's independence from Spanish domination with colorful parades, music, dancing, and fireworks. Plaza de Armas, the main plaza in Cusco, becomes the focus of the celebrations, drawing both residents and visitors. This is a fantastic chance to enjoy the lively Peruvian culture and indulge in traditional food from street vendors.

8. Traditional Music and Dance

Throughout the festivals, guests get the option to watch traditional Andean music and dance performances. The tunes of panpipes, drums, and string instruments fill the air as dancers demonstrate their abilities in bright costumes. Traditional dances like the Huayno and the Marinera are indicative of the region's cultural history and are performed with great pride and passion.

9. Local Crafts and Artisan Markets

Festivals in Cusco are also a good occasion to visit the city's artisan markets, where you may discover a vast assortment of handcrafted crafts, textiles, ceramics, and jewelry. These objects represent the region's rich creative heritage and provide for unique gifts to take back home.

10. Practical Tips for Tourists

When attending traditional festivals in Cusco, it's necessary to follow the local customs and traditions. Be wary about taking pictures during religious rituals, since certain events may be considered holy and private. Dress appropriately for the weather and be prepared for altitude sickness, since Cusco is situated at a high height. Additionally, arranging lodgings well in advance is essential, since events draw a substantial number of guests.

Peruvian Cuisine

Peruvian cuisine is a fascinating tapestry of tastes, merging indigenous ingredients with influences from Spanish, African, Chinese, and Japanese immigrants who have lived in the nation over the years. Cusco, as a gastronomic hotspot in Peru, gives guests a delightful voyage through the various and scrumptious meals that demonstrate the country's culinary diversity. From traditional meals that trace back to Inca times to current fusion concoctions, Peruvian cuisine in Cusco is an important experience for every food lover.

1. Introduction to Peruvian Cuisine in Cusco

Peruvian food has received worldwide praise in recent years, and Cusco is a fantastic spot to sample some of its best dishes. As the entryway to Machu Picchu and the core of the Andean region, Cusco possesses a gastronomic tradition inspired by the different ecosystems that surround it, from the highlands to the Amazon jungle. With ingredients like quinoa, potatoes, maize, and a multitude of unusual fruits and vegetables, Peruvian recipes are as varied as the landscapes they come from.

2. Staple Ingredients in Peruvian Cuisine

A basic component of Peruvian cuisine is its use of staple foods that have been farmed and enjoyed for millennia. Potatoes, native to the Andean area, come in different colors and sizes and are used in a number of cuisines, such as Papa a la Huancaina (potatoes in spicy cheese sauce) and Causa (layered potato dish). Quinoa, a superfood gaining popularity internationally, is another key component, commonly used in salads or as a replacement for rice.

3. Ceviche - Peru's Iconic Dish

No tour of Peruvian cuisine is complete without indulging in the country's most renowned dish - ceviche. Cusco, while not coastal, yet provides superb ceviche prepared with fresh fish or shellfish, marinated in lime juice, and seasoned with onions, chile peppers, and cilantro. The acidity of the lime "cooks" the raw fish, resulting in a delicious and tangy gastronomic pleasure that encapsulates the spirit of Peruvian seaside food.

4. Anticuchos - Grilled Perfection
Anticuchos, or skewered and grilled pork, are a famous street meal found across Peru. In Cusco, you'll find sellers grilling delicate and tasty beef heart (anticuchos de corazón) or chicken skewers. The meat is frequently marinated in a mix of spices and served with a side of potatoes or corn, providing a delightful combination of smoky and spicy aromas.

5. Alpaca and Guinea Pig - Traditional Andean Delicacies

For the adventurous gourmet, Cusco provides the option to taste traditional Andean delicacies like alpaca and guinea pig. Alpaca meat is thin, soft, and generally cooked as a steak or in stews, whereas guinea pig, or "cuy" as it is locally called, is often roasted whole and offered as a special meal during festivals or festivities.

6. Aji Gallina - Creamy and Spicy Comfort

Aji Gallina is a cosy Peruvian meal prepared with shredded chicken simmered in a rich and spicy yellow chili pepper sauce. The sauce is thickened with bread and milk, giving it a creamy texture, and is served with rice, boiled potatoes, and hard-boiled eggs. This rich and savoury meal is a perfect reflection of the combination of Peruvian and Spanish influences in the country's cuisine.

7. Chiriuchu - A Traditional Feast

Chiriuchu is a traditional cuisine that originated in Cusco and is commonly cooked at religious festivals and other events. It comprises of numerous Andean foods, including boiled potatoes, maize, cheese, rocoto pepper, seaweed, and dried meats like jerky. The arrangement of these elements on a plate is a piece of art, illustrating the harmony between the Andean and Incan traditions.

8. Pachamanca - Earth Oven Cooking

Pachamanca is an old Inca cooking method that includes preparing meat, potatoes, vegetables, and herbs in an earthen oven heated by hot stones. This unusual approach lends a distinct smokey taste to the foods, making it a must-try gastronomic experience in Cusco. Many restaurants in the city provide Pachamanca as part of their menu, enabling guests to partake in this traditional Andean feast.

9. Andean Desserts - A Sweet Finale

To satiate your sweet craving, Cusco offers a choice of scrumptious Andean delicacies. Alfajores, tiny shortbread biscuits filled with caramel (dulce de leche), are a popular dessert to enjoy. Queso Helado, or "frozen cheese," is a local ice cream flavoured with cinnamon and coconut, giving a new variation on the standard frozen delicacy. Picarones, sweet potato and pumpkin fritters sprinkled with sugar, make for a delightful street snack.

10. Peruvian Beverages - A Toast to Culture

Peru's unique topography and ecosystems give the right conditions for developing a broad variety of drinks. The nation is famed for its coffee and coca tea, the latter noted for its altitude-sickness alleviating effects. Pisco, a grape brandy, serves as the foundation for the national drink, Pisco Sour, a sour and foamy treat beloved across the country.

11. Fusion Cuisine and Modern Innovations

Cusco's culinary scene has expanded to include unique fusion meals that mix indigenous Peruvian ingredients with worldwide culinary trends. Many restaurants in the city provide inventive meals that merge local tastes with foreign influences, creating a unique and fascinating culinary experience for travellers seeking a modern take on traditional food.

12. Exploring Cusco's Food Markets

To properly comprehend the flavour of Peruvian cuisine, a visit to Cusco's busy food markets is a necessity. Mercado San Pedro is a dynamic centre where you can enjoy a range of local cuisines, fresh fruits, and traditional snacks. The market gives a real view into the everyday life of residents and the products that constitute the backbone of Peruvian culinary.

Local Arts and Crafts

Cusco, Peru, is not only recognised for its historical importance and magnificent surroundings but also for its flourishing arts and crafts sector. The city's rich cultural legacy, inspired by both Inca customs and Spanish colonisation, is vividly portrayed in the local arts and crafts. For travellers visiting Cusco, studying these creative representations is an immersing trip into the heart of Andean culture. From magnificent textiles to complex silverwork, Cusco's arts and crafts give an insight into the region's history, customs, and creative spirit.

1. Textiles - Weaving Traditions of the Andes

Textiles are a vital aspect of Andean culture, and Cusco is home to expert weavers who continue to maintain this old industry. Visitors may watch the ancient weaving process, from dyeing the fibers with natural substances like plants and minerals to utilising a backstrap loom to produce exquisite patterns and motifs. The Chinchero hamlet, situated near Cusco, is especially famous for its weaving traditions and gives a chance to acquire real, handcrafted textiles.

2. Alpaca and Vicuña Wool Products

Cusco is also a hotspot for alpaca and vicuña wool goods, showing the exquisite fibers created by these beautiful creatures endemic to the Andean area. Alpaca wool, famed for its softness and warmth, is used to manufacture scarves, sweaters, ponchos, and other comforting items. Vicuña wool, considered one of the finest and most costly fibers in the world, is used to manufacture stunning shawls and apparel items, expressing the exclusivity and refinement of Andean luxury.

3. Silverwork - Artistry in Metal

Peruvian artists have perfected the technique of silverwork, making magnificent jewelry and ornamental objects with complex patterns and themes. In Cusco's artisan markets, travellers may buy an assortment of silver jewelry, including necklaces, earrings, bracelets, and rings engraved with traditional Andean motifs and inspired by the region's natural beauty. The technique of silversmithing has strong roots in Cusco's history, extending back to the Inca civilisation, and continues to flourish as a vital component of the local artistic scene.

4. Pottery - Clay Creations

Pottery is another traditional art that has been handed down through centuries in Cusco. Traditional Andean pottery is recognised for its unique design and use of earthy hues. Artisans carefully mould and paint clay into different jars, sculptures, and figurines, frequently portraying animals, deities, and scenes from daily life. The pottery of Cusco represents the region's affinity with the ground and the devotion for Pachamama, the Inca Mother ground deity.

5. Wood Carvings - Expressions of Folk Art

Cusco's wood carvings are wonderful examples of folk art, featuring religious figures, animals, and mystical entities. Skilled carvers employ methods that have been developed over years to produce elaborate and detailed patterns on wooden sculptures, masks, and ornamental objects. The wood used frequently originates from the quenua tree, a native Andean species that contributes to the authenticity and value of the art.

6. Paintings and Art Galleries

Cusco's creative skill extends beyond painting, and the city is home to various art galleries that present works by local painters. Many of the paintings represent images from the city's history, scenery, and everyday life. The brilliant colors and attention to detail in these artworks catch the soul of Cusco's cultural heritage. Visitors may browse galleries and art markets to uncover unique artefacts that represent the creative character of the area.

7. Retablos - Intricate Altarpieces
Retablos are miniature, portable altarpieces that serve as a reflection of Andean spirituality. These gorgeous wooden boxes include elaborate miniature sceneries of religious figures, festivals, and historical events, meticulously made with paint, clay, and other materials. Retablos are a magnificent combination of Andean and Catholic ideas, merging traditional features with sacred symbolism.

8. Musical Instruments - The Rhythm of Cusco
Cusco is a city filled with music, and tourists may discover a diversity of traditional musical

instruments. The charango, a little Andean guitar-like instrument, is a popular option, recognised for its vibrant tones and unusual design. Panpipes, known as zampoñas or antaras, are also commonly available and represent the old musical traditions of the Andes. Musically interested travellers may buy these instruments as souvenirs and even take them home as a remembrance of their cultural adventure.

9. Traditional Masks - Festive Expressions

Masks play a vital part in Andean festivals and ceremonies, and Cusco is home to a variety of ornamental masks used in dance performances and religious rites. The brilliant colors and elaborate patterns of these masks represent the joyful attitude and cultural symbolism linked with many festivals and events in the area.

10. Artisan Markets - Shopping for Souvenirs

Cusco's artisan marketplaces, such as the San Pedro Market and the Centro Artesanal Cusco, are treasure troves for travellers seeking original and handmade gifts. These markets provide a diverse selection of arts and crafts, allowing a chance to connect with local craftsmen and support their traditional workmanship.

Chapter 8: Outdoor Activities

Cusco, Peru, is not just a city rich in history and culture but also a destination for outdoor lovers seeking adventurous activities and stunning surroundings. Surrounded by the stunning Andean mountains, verdant valleys, and ancient ruins, Cusco provides a multitude of outdoor activities that appeal to a broad range of interests and ability levels. Whether it's hiking to Machu Picchu, experiencing the Sacred Valley, or partaking in adrenaline-pumping activities, travellers visiting Cusco will discover a plethora of outdoor experiences that will leave them with amazing memories.

1. Trekking to Machu Picchu - The Inca Trail and Beyond
One of the most renowned outdoor activities in Cusco is hiking to Machu Picchu, the ancient

Inca fortress located high in the Andes. The famous Inca Trail is a multi-day trip that takes trekkers through stunning landscapes, various ecosystems, and ancient Inca ruins before reaching the awe-inspiring Machu Picchu at dawn. For those wanting a less congested option, there are additional hiking routes, such as the Salkantay Trek and the Lares Trek, which also lead to the famed fortress.

2. The Sacred Valley - Exploring Ancient Ruins
The Sacred Valley of the Incas, situated just outside Cusco, is a treasure mine of archaeological sites and natural delights. Tourists may tour ruins like as Pisac and Ollantaytambo, marvel at the agricultural terraces and breathtaking panoramas, and immerse themselves in the rich history of the Inca civilisation. The Sacred Valley is also a great place for bicycle trips, giving a new and thrilling approach to experience its splendour.

3. Rainbow Mountain - Vinicunca

Rainbow Mountain, or Vinicunca as it is called locally, has become one of Cusco's most popular outdoor attractions. This beautiful mountain has a vivid display of minerals and sediments, producing a natural rainbow-like pattern. To reach the peak and view this unique phenomenon, travellers may start on a tough but rewarding trip that takes them past lonely Andean settlements and stunning scenery.

4. Rafting and Kayaking - Navigating the Rapids

For adventure lovers, Cusco offers exhilarating rafting and kayaking activities on the Urubamba River. The river runs through the Sacred Valley, producing Class III and Class IV rapids suited for both novices and expert paddlers. The adrenaline thrill and breathtaking landscape make these water activities a great way to discover the region's natural splendour.

5. Paragliding - Soaring over Cusco

Paragliding is an amazing way to view Cusco's scenery from a new perspective. Tourists may take tandem paragliding flights with expert instructors, gliding above the city and experiencing bird's-eye views of the surrounding mountains and valleys. The sensation of freedom and the adrenaline rush make paragliding an amazing outdoor adventure.

6. Horseback Riding - Equestrian Exploration

Horseback riding is a terrific way to see the landscape surrounding Cusco. Visitors may ride through stunning landscapes, visit local towns, and explore historic Inca monuments while connecting with their gentle steeds. Horseback riding trips are offered for all levels of skill, making it a terrific pastime for families and tourists of all ages.

7. Mountain Biking - Off-Road Excursions

Cusco's mountainous topography gives lots of opportunity for mountain bike aficionados to engage on off-road excursions. There are varied riding tracks, from hard descents through the Andean highlands to relaxing rides through gorgeous valleys and farmlands. Biking excursions sometimes involve visits to ancient sites and encounters with local residents, adding cultural components to the outdoor experience.

8. Ziplining - Flying over the Andean Skies

Ziplining in Cusco is an adrenaline-pumping opportunity to view the region's sceneries. Tourists may fly over the Andean air, floating from one platform to another and enjoying breathtaking views of the surrounding mountains and valleys. Ziplining trips are accessible in numerous locales, including the Sacred Valley and other neighbouring sites.

9. Camping and Stargazing - Connecting with Nature

Cusco's secluded and unspoiled settings provide fantastic chances for camping and stargazing. Spending a night beneath the starry Andean sky is a magnificent experience, enabling travellers to connect with nature and enjoy the grandeur of the cosmos. Camping excursions sometimes feature bonfires, traditional dinners, and tales about Andean mythology.

10. Birdwatching - A Haven for Avian Enthusiasts

Cusco's various habitats make it a sanctuary for birding aficionados. The area is home to several bird species, including the Andean condor, hummingbirds, and brilliantly colored parrots. Birdwatching excursions take guests to strategic sites where they may witness these fascinating species in their natural surroundings.

11. ATV Adventures - Off-Roading in the Andes

For a fast-paced adventure, travellers may go on ATV (All-Terrain Vehicle) rides that take them through mountainous Andean landscapes and off-the-beaten-path tracks. ATV experiences provide an exciting way to explore Cusco's surroundings, giving an adrenaline rush and magnificent vistas along the route.

12. Hot Springs and Thermal Baths - Relaxation in Nature

After a day of outdoor activities, travellers may rest in Cusco's natural hot springs and thermal baths. The neighbouring town of Aguas Calientes, nestled at the foot of Machu Picchu, is famed for its hot baths, giving a peaceful and refreshing experience among the Andean mountains.

Hiking and Trekking

Cusco, Peru, is a paradise for hikers and trekkers, drawing outdoor enthusiasts from across the globe with its awe-inspiring landscapes, historic monuments, and cultural importance. Surrounded by the gorgeous Andean highlands, Cusco provides a multitude of hiking and trekking possibilities that appeal to a broad range of interests and ability levels. From the world-famous Inca Trail to hidden treasures like the Ausangate Trek, Cusco's hiking paths give an immersive trip into the heart of the Andean area. For travellers seeking adventure, history, and beautiful vistas, Cusco's hiking and trekking experiences are unsurpassed.

1. The Inca Trail - An Iconic Journey to Machu Picchu
The Inca Trail is certainly the most renowned hiking trail in Cusco and one of the most famous in the world. This ancient road brings

trekkers through breathtaking Andean vistas, cloud forests, and a succession of remarkable Inca sites before concluding at the awe-inspiring Machu Picchu at daybreak. The famous Inca Trail is a four-day, three-night journey that needs prior scheduling owing to limited daily permits. It is a tough but extremely rewarding route, enabling hikers to follow the footsteps of the ancient Incas and arrive at the sun gate with a beautiful view of Machu Picchu.

2. The Salkantay Trek - An Alternative to the Inca Trail

For those seeking for an alternative to the Inca Trail, the Salkantay Trek is a good choice. This five-day walk brings hikers through different environments, from high mountain passes to lush lowlands and subtropical woods. The centrepiece of the Salkantay Trek is the majestic Salkantay Mountain, one of the highest peaks in the Andes. The hike culminates with a visit to Machu Picchu, presenting a different and as stunning route to the old fortress.

3. The Ausangate Trek - A Hidden Gem in the Andes

The Ausangate Trek is a hidden treasure, providing a demanding and isolated trekking adventure that leads trekkers around the enormous Ausangate Mountain. This six-day walk gives a chance to engage in the indigenous Quechua culture, experience traditional Andean towns, and view spectacular glacier lakes and snow-capped peaks. The Ausangate Trek is less crowded than the Inca Trail, making it a suitable alternative for people seeking quiet and natural surroundings.

4. Choquequirao Trek - The Lost City of the Incas

The Choquequirao walk is commonly regarded to as the "sister" walk to Machu Picchu, since it leads to another famous Inca monument. Choquequirao, known as the "Lost City of the Incas," is an ancient archaeological site that can only be accessed by foot. The hike to Choquequirao is tough but rewarding, allowing a chance to see lesser-known ruins and enjoy beautiful views of the Apurimac River gorge.

5. Lares Trek - Culture and Scenery
The Lares Trek is a blend of trekking and cultural discovery, as it takes hikers through traditional Andean settlements where inhabitants preserve their centuries-old way of life. This four-day walk gives a look into true Andean culture, enabling travellers to mingle with local people and watch traditional textile weaving. The hike culminates with a visit to the picturesque hamlet of Aguas Calientes before rising to Machu Picchu.

6. Huchuy Qosqo Trek - An Ancient Inca Trail

The Huchuy Qosqo Trek is a very short but enjoyable two-day journey that brings hikers to the lesser-known Inca site of Huchuy Qosqo. This ancient site exhibits spectacular Inca terraces and stone constructions, surrounded by gorgeous mountain surroundings. The walk provides a combination of history and environment, making it a good alternative for those with limited time or wanting a less challenging climb.

7. Rainbow Mountain - Vinicunca Hike

The Rainbow Mountain, or Vinicunca, is a natural beauty that has become one of the most popular hiking locations in Cusco. The walk to Rainbow peak leads hikers through high-altitude landscapes, where they may experience the bright hues of the peak, generated by a unique mix of minerals and sediments. Although the trek is tough owing to the high altitude, the spectacular splendour of the Rainbow Mountain makes it a must-visit location for daring tourists.

8. Multi-Day Trekking Adventures - Vilcabamba and Vilcanota Range

Cusco offers a choice of multi-day hiking activities for seasoned hikers seeking more lengthy and hard trips. The Vilcabamba Range and the Vilcanota Range are two hilly places that provide lesser-explored hiking trails with spectacular views, old ruins, and interactions with indigenous inhabitants. These off-the-beaten-path journeys allow a deeper connection with the Andean culture and environment.

9. One-Day Hiking Options - Pisaq, Moray, and Maras

For travellers with limited time or searching for one-day hiking alternatives, Cusco offers various excellent climbs. Pisaq, Moray, and Maras are popular places for day treks, each having distinct attractions like as Inca ruins, agricultural terraces, and salt mines. These shorter climbs allow a chance to explore the grandeur of the Andean area without committing to multi-day expeditions.

10. Essential Hiking Tips for Tourists

When beginning on hiking and trekking experiences in Cusco, it's vital to be prepared and knowledgeable. Tourists should acclimatise to the high altitude in Cusco before commencing any trip, remain hydrated, and pack important gear like as appropriate hiking shoes, rain gear, and warm clothes. Hiring an experienced guide is strongly advised, as they may give unique insights into the region's history, culture, and natural beauty while assuring safety throughout the walk.

Rafting and Kayaking

Cusco, Peru, is not only a city rich in history and culture but also a heaven for adventure enthusiasts. Surrounded by the breathtaking Andean scenery and passed by the great Urubamba River, Cusco offers exhilarating rafting and kayaking adventures for travellers wishing to push themselves and immerse in the natural beauty of the area. Whether navigating over Class III and IV rapids or quietly paddling on calmer stretches of the river, Cusco's rafting and kayaking activities guarantee adrenaline-pumping thrill and magnificent surroundings.

1. Rafting in Cusco - An Adrenaline Rush on the Urubamba River

Rafting on the Urubamba River is one of the most popular adventure sports in Cusco. The river runs through the Sacred Valley, giving a fantastic location for both novices and expert rafts. The Urubamba River is separated into numerous parts, each having varied degrees of difficulty, from Class I to Class V rapids. The Class III and Class IV portions give an exciting ride, with adrenaline-pumping waves and dramatic drops that provide an amazing rafting experience.

2. The Balsas Section - An Ideal Adventure for Beginners

The Balsas portion of the Urubamba River is suitable for novices and families wanting a rafting experience. This segment offers Class I to Class II rapids, giving a combination of smooth stretches and modest waves, excellent for first-time rafters or those wishing for a more peaceful rafting experience. The Balsas portion lets people to appreciate the surrounding environment and examine the local flora and animals while floating along the river.

3. The Chuquicahuana (Chuqui) Section - Thrilling Rapids and Stunning Scenery

The Chuqui stretch of the Urubamba River is noted for its Class III and Class IV rapids, making it an exciting alternative for more experienced rafters. This segment takes guests through the difficult terrain of the Sacred Valley, affording stunning vistas of the Andean highlands and possibilities to visit Inca sites along the riverbanks. The mix of hard rapids and magnificent surroundings makes the Chuqui segment an amazing rafting excursion.

4. Multi-Day Rafting Expeditions - Remote River Exploration

For those wanting a longer rafting trip, multi-day adventures are offered, bringing participants on a trek through isolated and lesser-explored areas of the Urubamba River. These multi-day tours allow a deeper immersion in the natural marvels of the area, as rafters sleep along the riverbanks and eat meals provided by the guide crew. These treks are suitable for adventure enthusiasts who seek to unplug from the contemporary world and explore the wildness of the Andes.

5. Kayaking in Cusco - Paddling through the Andean Rapids

Cusco's kayaking chances are great for anyone wanting a more intimate and difficult journey. Kayakers may explore the Urubamba River and its numerous portions, taking on Class III and Class IV rapids with accuracy and expertise. Kayaking enables participants to have a deeper connection to the river, as they manoeuvre through the waves and dips, enjoying the surge of adrenaline and the beauty of the Andean landscapes.

6. Professional Guides and Safety Measures

When partaking in rafting and kayaking excursions in Cusco, safety is of greatest concern. Reputable tour providers offer competent guides who are skilled in river navigation and first aid. These trained guides ensure that participants have the proper equipment, including life jackets and helmets, and get complete safety briefings before beginning on the expedition. With safety as a key concern, travellers can enjoy their rafting and kayaking excursions with confidence and peace of mind.

7. Combining Adventure with Culture

One of the unique characteristics of rafting and kayaking in Cusco is the possibility to mix action with cultural experiences. Many rafting and kayaking programmes include visits to traditional Andean settlements along the riverbanks, enabling guests to learn about local customs, traditions, and ways of life. These cultural connections strengthen the whole experience, offering a better awareness for the region's history and legacy.

8. Rafting and Kayaking Season in Cusco

The greatest time for rafting and kayaking in Cusco is during the dry season, which normally stretches from May to September. During this month, the river levels are lower, offering more bearable conditions for both novices and experienced explorers. The water is also clearer, offering improved sight and increasing the whole experience. While rafting and kayaking may be enjoyed at other seasons of the year, it's vital to check with local tour operators regarding current conditions and safety procedures.

9. Responsible Tourism and Environmental Conservation

Cusco's outdoor experiences take place in the heart of the Andean highlands, a sensitive habitat with distinct biodiversity. It is crucial for travellers and tour operators to conduct responsible tourism and environmental protection to safeguard these natural beauties. This involves following to Leave No Trace principles, respecting local people and their traditions, and reducing the effect on the environment while enjoying these wonderful outdoor activities.

10. Essential Tips for Rafting and Kayaking Tourists

Before starting on a rafting or kayaking experience in Cusco, travellers should consider the following tips:

- Be physically healthy and prepared for physical effort, particularly for more tough stretches of the river.

- Dress correctly in comfortable and quick-drying gear that may become wet throughout the activity. - Wear sunscreen and a hat to protect against the intense Andean sun.

- Bring a waterproof camera or a GoPro to record the spectacular experiences on the river.

- Listen attention to the guides' instructions and obey safety recommendations at all times.

- Respect the natural environment and the local communities encountered throughout the expedition.

Mountain Biking

Cusco, Peru, is a mountain biking paradise for daring travellers seeking exhilarating rides, magnificent scenery, and a unique way to experience the Andean country. Surrounded by the spectacular Andes Mountains and crossed by historic trails and off-road pathways, Cusco offers a choice of mountain biking adventures that appeal to all skill levels and interests. From adrenaline-pumping descents to relaxing rides through gorgeous valleys, mountain biking in Cusco offers a memorable experience into the heart of the Andes.

1. Mountain Biking in Cusco - A Thrilling Adventure

Mountain riding in Cusco gives an adrenaline-pumping and immersive trip across the rocky terrain of the Andes. The region's diversified topography provides a combination of demanding descents, technical trails, and picturesque routes that display the natural beauty and cultural legacy of the area. For travellers seeking an athletic and interesting way to see the Andean area, mountain biking in Cusco is a must-do activity.

2. Bike Rental and Tour Options

Tourists may discover a selection of bike rental businesses in Cusco that provide high-quality mountain bikes ideal for various kinds of terrain and riding tastes. Additionally, there are numerous tour companies that give guided mountain biking experiences, catering to different skill levels and interests. Whether it's a half-day trail ride or an extended multi-day trip, travellers may pick from a number of alternatives to fit their interests and timetables.

3. Sacsayhuaman and Puka Pukara Circuit - A Historical Ride

For an exhilarating mountain riding adventure paired with a historical tour, the Sacsayhuaman and Puka Pukara Circuit is an ideal option. This path brings bicyclists past historic Inca monuments, including the spectacular Sacsayhuaman castle and the archaeological complex of Puka Pukara. The course provides a combination of dirt roads and single tracks, delivering a unique mixture of history and excitement.

4. Maras and Moray - Exploring Salt Mines and Agricultural Terraces

The Maras and Moray route is a famous mountain biking track that brings travellers through the scenic Sacred Valley. The journey includes a visit to the interesting Maras Salt Mines, where salt has been collected since Inca times, and the Inca agricultural terraces of

Moray. This picturesque journey enables riders to immerse themselves in the region's agricultural history while enjoying spectacular views of the surrounding surroundings.

5. Chinchero to Ollantaytambo - A Scenic Andean Journey

The track from Chinchero to Ollantaytambo is a picturesque mountain bike route that goes into the centre of the Andean highlands. Bikers will ride through traditional Andean villages, meet local residents, and see the timeless grandeur of the Andes. The trek culminates in the historic village of Ollantaytambo, where travellers may see the spectacular Inca ruins and recover before further activities.

6. Abra Malaga - A Thrilling Downhill Descent

For adrenaline enthusiasts wanting an amazing downhill descent, the Abra Malaga course is a must-try activity. This journey starts in the high mountain pass of Abra Malaga, descending through beautiful scenery, cloud forests, and verdant lowlands. The exhilarating descent concludes in the municipality of Santa Maria, delivering an amazing and adrenaline-pumping adventure.

7. Lares Valley - A Multi-Day Mountain Biking Expedition

For a more longer and immersive mountain riding experience, the Lares Valley offers a multi-day trip through rugged Andean landscapes and traditional towns. The Lares Valley route enables bicyclists to visit lesser-known sections of the Andes, creating a closer connection with the region's natural beauty and cultural legacy.

8. Mountain Biking Safety and Precautions

Before beginning on a mountain bike journey in Cusco, travellers should consider the following safety guidelines and precautions:

- Wear proper safety gear, including a helmet, gloves, and knee pads.
- Dress in layers to suit changeable weather conditions in the Andes. - Stay hydrated and bring adequate water for the ride.
- Bring a map or GPS device and acquaint yourself with the trail path.
- Listen attention to the guide's instructions and follow their recommendations throughout the journey.
- Be mindful of local animals and appreciate the natural environment.

9. Responsible Tourism and Environmental Conservation

Mountain biking in Cusco takes occur in environmentally vulnerable places, and it is necessary for travellers and tour operators to adopt responsible tourism and environmental protection. This involves following to Leave No Trace principles, respecting local people and their traditions, and reducing the effect on the environment while enjoying these wonderful outdoor activities.

10. Mountain Biking Events and Competitions

Cusco holds various mountain bike events and contests throughout the year, drawing athletes from across the globe. These events vary from simple rides to tough races, allowing travellers the chance to experience the strong mountain biking culture of the area and connect with other riding aficionados.

11. Essential Tips for Mountain Biking Tourists

Before going on a mountain bike journey in Cusco, travellers should consider the following tips:

- Ensure that your mountain bike talents fit the difficulty level of the selected path.
- Check the weather prediction and be prepared for shifting circumstances.

- Bring a small backpack with basics such as water, food, a first-aid kit, and a camera.

- Respect the local communities and their culture throughout the journey.

- Consider hiring a local guide who is acquainted with the landscape and can give insights into the region's history and culture.

Chapter 9: Practical Information

Practical knowledge is crucial for travellers considering a vacation to Cusco, Peru. From travel advice and transit alternatives to currency, health, and safety issues, having a thorough awareness of practical facts may improve the whole travel experience and guarantee a smooth and pleasurable journey. In this detailed guide, we will cover all the practical facts that travellers need to know before visiting Cusco.

1. Travel Documents and Visa Requirements

Before coming to Cusco, travellers should check they have all the proper travel papers. Citizens of several countries may visit Peru without a visa for tourist reasons, often for a term of up to 90 days. However, visa requirements may vary dependent on the traveler's nationality, therefore it is crucial to verify the exact requirements for your place of origin well in advance of your journey.

Tourists should also confirm that their passport is valid for at least six months beyond their scheduled date of departure from Peru. It is suggested to carry a duplicate of the passport's information page and preserve it separately from the original document.

2. Vaccinations and Health Precautions

Before flying to Cusco, it is suggested to see a healthcare expert or a travel medicine clinic to receive information on essential vaccines and health precautions. Some tourists may need immunisations for illnesses such as yellow fever, typhoid, and hepatitis A and B. Additionally, altitude sickness is a risk for travellers coming in Cusco owing to its high height. Tourists are urged to take it easy upon arriving, consume lots of water, and avoid excessive alcohol intake.

3. Altitude Sickness and Acclimatization

Cusco stands at a height of roughly 3,400 meters (11,150 feet) above sea level, while the surrounding area contains much higher peaks. Altitude sickness, commonly known as soroche, is a major issue for travellers arriving in Cusco. Symptoms might vary from slight pain to serious health difficulties.

To avoid the danger of altitude sickness, travellers are encouraged to spend at least a day acclimatizing in Cusco before indulging in vigorous activities. Avoiding considerable physical effort during the first 24 to 48 hours, drinking lots of water, and avoiding alcohol and heavy meals may also aid in acclimation. If symptoms of altitude sickness grow severe, obtaining medical assistance is necessary.

4. Best Time to Visit Cusco

Cusco's temperature fluctuates according on the season, thus the ideal time to visit depends on individual tastes and planned activities. The dry season, from May to September, is typically regarded the ideal period for tourism, since the weather is mostly dry, and the sky are clear, giving good conditions for sightseeing and outdoor sports.

The rainy season, from November to March, is marked by regular rains and occasional difficulties in travel owing to mudslides and road closures. However, the rainy season also produces beautiful green vistas and is an excellent time for photographers and people interested in agricultural beauty.

5. Currency and Money Matters

The official currency of Peru is the Peruvian Sol (PEN). ATMs are extensively accessible in Cusco, and credit cards are commonly accepted at most hotels, restaurants, and tourism enterprises. However, it is good to carry some cash in small denominations for purchases at smaller businesses and while visiting markets.

It is crucial to tell your bank of your trip intentions to Peru before your departure to prevent any complications with using your credit or debit cards overseas.

6. Language and Communication

Spanish is the official language of Peru, and it is extensively spoken in Cusco. While English is spoken in many tourist locations, learning some basic Spanish phrases might be beneficial for conversing with locals, particularly in more isolated places.

Wi-Fi is provided in most hotels, restaurants, and cafés in Cusco, making it simple for travellers to remain connected. Tourists may also acquire local SIM cards for their phones to have access to data and make local calls.

7. Transportation in Cusco

Cusco has a well-developed transportation network that makes it simple for travellers to explore the city and its surrounds. Taxis are available and reasonably reasonable inside the city. It is advisable to negotiate the fee before getting into the cab or utilise ride-sharing applications for increased convenience.

For greater distances, travellers may go by bus or arrange for private trips to famous places like Machu Picchu, the Sacred Valley, and other local sights.

8. Safety and Security

Cusco is a fairly secure city for travellers, but as in other trip location, it is vital to take some safety precautions. Tourists should avoid exhibiting precious objects in public, be vigilant with their possessions in busy locations, and avoid strolling alone late at night.

It is also important to employ certified tour operators and transportation services to provide a safe and fun experience on excursions and adventures.

9. Local Customs and Respect for Culture

Peruvians are typically warm and welcoming, and it is necessary for visitors to show respect for the local culture and traditions. When visiting churches or religious places, dress modestly and adhere to any special regulations or standards. It is courteous to ask for permission before shooting images of people or local communities.

10. Electricity and Plugs

Peru employs 220-volt electrical outlets with two circular prongs (Type C and Type A plugs). Tourists from countries employing a different voltage or plug type should carry necessary adapters and converters for their electrical equipment.

11. Shopping and Souvenirs

Cusco is noted for its bustling markets, selling a range of handicrafts, textiles, jewelry, and other goods. Tourists can tour marketplaces like the San Pedro Market and the Centro Artesanal Cusco to acquire unique goods to take home as keepsakes of their vacation.

12. Dress Code and Weather Considerations

Cusco's weather may be varied, therefore it is vital to carry clothes suited for diverse circumstances. Layers are essential, since temperatures may change greatly between day and night. Comfortable walking shoes are an essential for touring the city and its neighbouring attractions.

When visiting holy locations, modest dress is appropriate, and it may be essential to cover shoulders and knees.

13. Emergency Contact Information

Before visiting to Cusco, travellers should make note of emergency contact information, including the local police, hospitals, and their country's embassy or consulate in Peru. Having this knowledge readily accessible might be beneficial in case of any unanticipated occurrences.

Accommodation Options

Cusco, Peru's historical treasure and the entrance to the famed Machu Picchu, draws millions of travellers every year. The city's rich history, lively culture, and gorgeous architecture make it a must-visit destination. When planning a vacation to Cusco, selecting the proper hotel is vital to guarantee a pleasant and pleasurable stay. This thorough guide analyses numerous housing alternatives in Cusco, ranging from budget-friendly hostels to expensive hotels, to assist travellers make educated selections that best fit their interests and budget.

1. Hotels:

Cusco provides a broad choice of hotels, from quaint boutique accommodations to opulent 5-star ones. Hotels are a popular alternative for travellers seeking comfort and convenience, and many provide spectacular views of the city and surrounding countryside. Some top-rated hotels in Cusco include:

a) Belmond Palacio Nazarenas: This 5-star hotel oozes grandeur and elegance, with large rooms, a quiet courtyard, and a heated outdoor pool. Located in the centre of Cusco, it gives convenient access to famous sites.

b) JW Marriott El Convento Cusco: Housed in a magnificently renovated 16th-century convent, this upmarket hotel mixes history with contemporary conveniences. Guests may enjoy the on-site spa and gourmet eateries.

c) Casa Cartagena Boutique Hotel & Spa: Nestled in a historic home, this boutique hotel provides a customised and private experience. The spa facilities and verdant grounds contribute to the overall peacefulness.

2. Hostels:

For budget-conscious tourists, hostels in Cusco give a cost-effective and social housing choice. Hostels are numerous throughout the city, particularly in the San Blas district, catering to travellers and lone visitors. Popular hostels include:

a) Loki Hostel Cusco: Known for its vibrant environment and social activities, Loki Hostel is a terrific spot to meet other travelers. It has a rooftop bar with amazing city views.

b) Wild Rover Backpackers: Located in the centre of Cusco, this hostel provides comfortable dormitory and private accommodation choices, along with a dynamic on-site bar.

c) Pariwana Hostel Cusco: Combining comfort with a sociable setting, Pariwana Hostel provides common spaces, a vibrant bar, and frequent activities, making it perfect for meeting new people.

3. Bed and Breakfasts:

For a more personal experience, travellers may pick bed & breakfast lodgings in Cusco. These places frequently feature a comfortable environment, home-cooked meals, and individualised attention. Some suggested B&Bs include:

a) Amaru Inca: Situated in a peaceful region, Amaru Inca provides delightful rooms furnished with classic Inca-style décor. The pleasant personnel and cooked breakfast add to its charm.

b) El Balcón: This family-run B&B overlooks the main plaza, Plaza de Armas, affording visitors with beautiful views of the city's attractions. The warm hosts make tourists feel perfectly at home.

c) La Casa de Mayte: Located in the San Blas area, this B&B provides pleasant rooms and a tranquil patio. The excellent breakfast incorporates local foods.

4. Vacation Rentals:

Tourists searching for a home-away-from-home experience might choose for holiday rentals in Cusco. These residences vary from small flats to huge villas, appealing to families and groups. Websites like Airbnb and Vrbo give several possibilities for holiday rentals in Cusco.

5. Eco-Lodges:

For eco-conscious guests, Cusco boasts numerous eco-lodges that promote sustainability and provide immersive natural experiences. These lodges are often situated in the Sacred Valley, allowing tourists the option to engage with the natural environment. Some prominent eco-lodges are:

a) Inkaterra Hacienda Urubamba: Situated in the Sacred Valley, this eco-lodge has exquisite rooms with spectacular mountain views and organic gardens.

b) Explora Valle Sagrado: Focused on sustainable practices, Explora provides guided trips to lesser-known destinations, delivering a genuine Peruvian experience.

Local Transportation

Cusco, the ancient capital of the Inca Empire and a UNESCO World Heritage Site, provides a plethora of cultural and natural attractions for travellers to discover. Getting about the city and its surrounds effectively and comfortably is crucial to make the most of your vacation. This thorough guide includes full information on the numerous local transportation alternatives accessible to visitors in Cusco, including buses, taxis, rental vehicles, and other forms of transit.

1. Public Buses:

Public buses are the most economical and readily accessible means of local transportation in Cusco. The city has a comprehensive network of bus lines linking key attractions, neighborhoods, and the city center. The buses are clearly distinguishable by their bright exteriors and run from early morning until late at night.

a) Cusco Bus station: The major bus station, Terminal Terrestre Cusco, is situated roughly 15 minutes from the city center via cab. It serves as the departure and arrival point for buses heading to numerous places inside Cusco and beyond, including adjacent towns and tourist spots.

b) Fare and Payment: Bus prices in Cusco are affordable, with set rates for most routes. It is recommended to bring modest change, since certain buses may not take big amounts.

c) **Safety:** While public buses are typically safe, travellers should be wary about pickpocketing and keep a watch on their valuables during busy hours.

2. Taxis:

Taxis are a practical and commonly accessible choice for commuting about Cusco, particularly for shorter distances or while going during late hours. Tourists may hail a cab on the street or locate one at approved taxi stops.

a) **Taxi Rates:** Taxis in Cusco do not use meters, thus it is vital to negotiate the fee before commencing the ride. It is a good idea to ask locals or your accommodation provider about the usual rate to your location to prevent overcharging.

b) Safety: For safety reasons, it is advisable to utilise licenced taxis, identified by their official signs and license plates. Trusted cab applications like Uber and Cabify are also accessible in Cusco and give transparent pricing.

3. Car Rentals:

For travellers who prefer the option of exploring at their own leisure, automobile rentals are available in Cusco. Renting a vehicle enables guests to drive beyond the city boundaries and experience the breathtaking scenery of the Sacred Valley and other local sites.

a) Requirements: To hire a vehicle in Cusco, travellers must produce a valid driver's license, passport, and a credit card for security deposit reasons.

b) Road Conditions: While major highways are well-maintained, certain rural roads might be narrow and twisting. It is necessary to drive safely and be informed of local traffic restrictions.

c) Parking: Finding parking in the city center may be problematic, therefore it is advised to check with your hotel about parking availability or utilise public parking lots.

4. Alternative Transportation:

Apart from typical forms of transportation, Cusco provides unique choices that contribute to the whole tourist experience:

a) Walking: Cusco's tiny city core is best experienced on foot. Walking enables travellers to immerse themselves in the exquisite colonial buildings, find secret passageways, and stumble upon local markets and cafés.

b) Biking: Cycling lovers may explore Cusco and its surrounds by hiring bikes. Several bike tour organisations offer guided trips, including routes to ancient sites and the Sacred Valley.

c) Horseback Riding: For a really immersive experience, travellers may choose for horseback riding trips that take them through the gorgeous countryside and historic Inca pathways.

d) Train: When visiting the famed Machu Picchu, travellers may take the picturesque train trip from Cusco or Ollantaytambo to Aguas Calientes, the entrance to the historic Inca fortress.

Safety Tips

Cusco, Peru's ancient treasure and the entrance to the spectacular Machu Picchu, draws millions of travellers from across the globe each year. While Cusco provides a variety of cultural and natural treasures, it's crucial for guests to emphasise safety throughout their stay. This thorough book offers travellers with practical safety guidelines to guarantee a comfortable and happy experience while experiencing Cusco and its surrounds.

1. Pre-Trip Preparation:

a) study: Before going to Cusco, undertake comprehensive study on the region, including local traditions, culture, and safety issues. Understanding the area's topography and meteorological conditions might help you prepare correctly.

b) Travel Insurance: Invest in comprehensive travel insurance that covers medical emergencies, trip cancellations, and theft.

Confirm that it provides coverage for outdoor activities, like as hiking or adventure sports.

c) immunisations: Check with your healthcare practitioner about recommended immunisations for Peru and the area, and ensure you are up-to-date with regular vaccinations.

2. Personal Safety:

a) Be Mindful of Valuables: Avoid bringing extra cash, jewelry, or valuable devices. Use a money belt or a disguised bag to keep vital papers and money secure.

b) Split Belongings: Divide your cash and cards, putting them in various areas to minimize loss in case of theft.

c) Secure lodgings: Choose reputed lodgings with secure access and safes in the room to keep valuables while you are not using them.

d) Stay Alert in busy Areas: Be alert in busy locations like marketplaces and tourist destinations, since these may be hotspots for pickpocketing. Keep your valuables nearby and be mindful of your surroundings.

e) Use Reputable Transportation: Opt for licenced taxis or transportation providers suggested by your hotel. Avoid unmarked cars and taxis without proper signage.

f) Avoid wandering Alone at Night: While Cusco is typically secure, it is advised to avoid wandering alone in poorly lit or unknown places, particularly after midnight.

3. Cultural Sensitivity:

a) Dress Respectfully: Cusco is a city with deep-rooted traditions and traditional attitudes. Dress modestly while visiting religious places and local communities to show respect for their culture.

b) Learn Basic Spanish Phrases: While English is spoken in tourist regions, knowing some basic Spanish phrases will aid with communication and build a pleasant contact with locals.

c) Respect Local Customs: Observe and respect local customs, including photography prohibitions in some locations and obtaining permission before photographing individuals.

4. Altitude Sickness:

a) Gradual Acclimatization: Cusco stands at an altitude of nearly 3,000 meters (10,000 feet), and altitude sickness might afflict certain travellers. Take it gently on your first day to enable your body to acclimatise gradually.

b) remain Hydrated: Drink lots of water to remain hydrated and avoid alcohol and caffeine, since these may increase altitude-related symptoms.

c) medicine: Consult your doctor about altitude sickness medicine and carry required medication if prescribed.

5. Food and Water Safety:

a) Safe Food measures: Eat at reputed restaurants and food vendors with good sanitary measures. Avoid ingesting raw or undercooked meals and fruits or vegetables washed in tap water.

b) Bottled Water: Drink only bottled or boiling water to avoid waterborne diseases.

6. Adventure Activities:

a) Choose Licensed Tour Operators: When indulging in adventure sports, such as hiking or mountain biking, pick licensed and reputed tour operators with competent guides.

b) Check Safety Equipment: Ensure that safety equipment, such as helmets and harnesses, is supplied and in excellent condition before engaging in any adventure activity.

7. Machu Picchu Visits:

a) Tickets and permissions: Secure your Machu Picchu admission ticket and any needed permissions well in advance, since daily visitor numbers are restricted.

b) Guided Tours: Consider hiring an expert guide to improve your Machu Picchu experience and acquire significant insights into the site's history and importance.

Language and Communication

Cusco, the ancient capital of the Inca Empire and a UNESCO World Heritage Site, draws millions of visitors from across the world. While Spanish is the official language of Cusco, the city's rich cultural legacy and strong tourist economy ensure that conversation in many languages is frequent. This thorough book offers travellers with crucial information on the linguistic situation in Cusco, typical phrases in Spanish, local customs, and advice for efficient communication to improve their trip experience.

1. Language Situation in Cusco:

a) Official Language: Spanish is the official language of Peru and is extensively spoken throughout Cusco. It is the predominant language used in government, education, and media.

b) Indigenous Languages: In addition to Spanish, Cusco is home to various indigenous languages, including Quechua and Aymara. While these languages are not as often spoken in metropolitan areas, they play a crucial role in rural communities.

c) English: English is the most often spoken foreign language in Cusco's tourist regions. Many hotel employees, tour guides, and merchants have basic to excellent English language abilities to cater to foreign guests.

2. Basic Spanish Phrases:

Learning some simple Spanish words may tremendously boost communication and engagement with locals. Here are crucial terms for tourists:

a) Greetings: "Hola" (Hello), "Buenos días" (Good morning), "Buenas tardes" (Good afternoon), "Buenas noches" (Good evening/night).

b) Polite Phrases: "Por favor" (Please), "Gracias" (Thank you), "De nada" (You're welcome), "Disculpe" or "Perdón" (Excuse me, Pardon me).

c) Numbers: Knowing numbers is important for shopping and negotiating costs. "Uno"

(One), "dos" (Two), "tres" (Three), "cuatro" (Four), "cinco" (Five), "diez" (Ten).

d) Asking for Help: "¿Dónde está...?" (Where is...?), "Necesito ayuda" (I need aid), "No entiendo" (I don't understand).

e) Ordering Food: "Quisiera..." (I would like...), "La cuenta, por favor" (The bill, please).

3. Communication Tips:

a) Speak Slowly and properly: When conversing in Spanish, speak slowly and enunciate properly to enhance comprehension, particularly if you are not proficient.

b) Use motions and Visuals: Incorporate motions and visuals to deliver your point effectively. Pointing to items or using hand gestures might be useful.

c) Smile and Be Polite: A warm manner and a smile may go a long way in creating great relationships with locals.

d) Learn Local phrases: Familiarize yourself with local phrases and greetings to show respect for the culture and connect with people.

4. Quechua and Aymara:

a) Cultural importance: Quechua and Aymara are indigenous languages with great cultural importance. Learning simple greetings or words in these languages might be appreciated by locals, particularly in rural locations.

b) Greetings in Quechua: "Allin kawsay" (Good morning), "Allin p'unchay" (Good afternoon), "Allin tuta" (Good evening).

5. Language Apps & Translation Tools:

a) Language applications: Use language study applications like Duolingo, Babbel, or Rosetta Stone to brush up on Spanish before your trip.

b) Translation Tools: Translation programmes like Google Translate may be beneficial for on-the-spot translations.

6. Cultural Sensitivity:

a) Respect Local conventions: Embrace local conventions and norms, and be attentive to cultural differences when speaking with locals.

b) Addressing Locals: When addressing locals, use formal pronouns such "usted" (you) to demonstrate respect, particularly with elderly folks or those in positions of power.

7. English-Speaking Services:

a) Tour Guides: Many tour guides in Cusco provide services in English and other languages. Hiring a tour may increase your awareness of the city's history and legacy.

b) Accommodations: Hotels and hostels generally offer English-speaking employees, making it easy to obtain help and information.

Chapter 10: Cusco's Surroundings

Nestled in the Andes Mountains of Peru, Cusco is a city rich in history, culture, and natural beauty. Beyond the city's unique attractions, Cusco's environs offer an assortment of magnificent scenery, historic ruins, colourful marketplaces, and traditional communities ready to be visited by travellers. This thorough book gives critical information on the key sites in Cusco's surrounds, including the Sacred Valley, Machu Picchu, Rainbow Mountain, Maras, Moray, and the Amazon Rainforest, providing travellers a varied and fascinating experience.

1. The Sacred Valley:

a) Overview: The Sacred Valley, commonly known as the Urubamba Valley, is a scenic landscape running along the Urubamba River.

It is filled with old Inca ruins, terraced slopes, and lovely communities, making it a must-visit destination for history buffs and environment lovers.

b) Pisac: The town of Pisac is recognised for its thriving artisan market, providing a broad range of crafts, textiles, and jewelry. The Pisac Ruins hang high above the town, presenting amazing Inca architecture and panoramic vistas.

c) Ollantaytambo: This well-preserved Inca village contains spectacular stone terraces and buildings, notably the enormous Temple of the Sun. Ollantaytambo is also the starting point for many Machu Picchu-bound rail itineraries.

d) Chinchero: Known for its colorful Sunday market, Chinchero is a terrific site to explore traditional Andean culture and observe the expert weavers at work.

e) Moray: The intriguing archaeological site of Moray comprises of remarkable concentric terraces that were utilised for agricultural experiments by the Incas.

f) Maras Salt Mines: The spectacular salt evaporation ponds of Maras have been in use since Inca times, and the complex patterns they generate are a photographer's joy.

2. Machu Picchu:

a) Overview: One of the New Seven Wonders of the World, Machu Picchu is an old Inca fortress located high in the Andes Mountains. It delivers an awe-inspiring experience with its beautiful stone architecture and stunning panoramas.

b) Getting to Machu Picchu: Tourists may reach Machu Picchu by taking a train from

Cusco or Ollantaytambo to Aguas Calientes, followed by a bus journey to the entrance of the ancient site. Alternatively, travellers might go for the arduous Inca Trail trip.

c) Huayna Picchu and Machu Picchu Mountain: For more daring guests, climbing Huayna Picchu or Machu Picchu Mountain gives unrivalled views of the citadel and the surrounding mountains.

d) Guided Tours: Consider hiring a qualified guide to learn about Machu Picchu's history and importance, since they may give useful insights.

3. Rainbow Mountain (Vinicunca):

a) Overview: The Rainbow Mountain, or Vinicunca, is a natural marvel situated at high altitude in the Peruvian Andes. Its distinctive hues, generated by the mineral deposits in the rocks, attract hikers and environment lovers.

b) Trekking to Rainbow peak: The trip to Rainbow Mountain is tough owing to high altitude, but the breathtaking vistas of the multi-colored peak make it a worthwhile experience.

c) Acclimatization: To avoid the symptoms of altitude sickness, spend a few days acclimatizing in Cusco before trying the journey.

4. The Amazon Rainforest:

a) Overview: A visit to the Amazon Rainforest is a once-in-a-lifetime chance to immerse oneself in one of the most biodiverse ecosystems on Earth.

b) Puerto Maldonado or Iquitos: From Cusco, tourists may fly to Puerto Maldonado or Iquitos to reach the Amazon Rainforest. Both areas offer great eco-lodges and guided excursions.

c) species and Nature: In the Amazon, tourists may witness a broad assortment of species, including monkeys, colorful birds, caimans, and enormous river otters. Guided hikes and boat cruises allow opportunity to learn about the different flora and animals.

5. Tipon and Pikillaqta:

a) Tipon: The archaeological site of Tipon has outstanding Inca terraces and intricate irrigation systems, a monument to the Incas' technical ability.

b) Pikillaqta: This large pre-Inca archaeological site has ancient adobe constructions and is considered to have been an administrative hub.

Rainbow Mountain

Nestled high in the Andes Mountains in Cusco, Peru, Rainbow Mountain, commonly known as Vinicunca, is a natural beauty that has captured the hearts of people from across the world. Its bright and surreal hues, generated by mineral deposits in the rocks, have given it the moniker "Rainbow Mountain." This thorough book gives crucial information for travellers eager to embark on an amazing adventure to this awe-inspiring place. From trekking recommendations to acclimatization, local culture, and the ideal time to visit, this book covers all you need to know to make the most of your trip at Rainbow Mountain.

1. Location & Geography:

a) Rainbow Mountain is situated around 100 kilometers southeast of Cusco, near the Ausangate Mountain, the highest mountain in the area.

b) Situated at a height of roughly 5,200 meters (17,060 feet) above sea level, the trip to Rainbow Mountain may be physically taxing owing to the high elevation.

c) The unusual hues of Rainbow Mountain are a consequence of iron oxide, copper sulfide, and other minerals contained in the rock strata.

2. Planning Your Trip:

a) greatest Time to Visit: The greatest time to visit Rainbow Mountain is during the dry season from April to October. The weather is often clear, affording beautiful vistas of the mountain's brilliant colours.

b) Weather Conditions: The weather in the Andes may be unpredictable, especially during the dry season. It is necessary to be prepared for rapid changes in temperature and meteorological conditions.

c) Acclimatization: Given the high altitude of Rainbow Mountain, acclimatization is necessary to prevent altitude sickness. Spend a few days in Cusco or other high-altitude locales before trying the journey.

d) Permits and Guided Tours: To visit Rainbow Mountain, it is required to get a trekking permit. Guided tours are strongly advised, since expert guides are knowledgeable with the terrain and can assure your safety.

3. Trekking to Rainbow Mountain:

a) Difficulty Level: The trip to Rainbow Mountain is classified moderate to tough owing to the high altitude and steep inclines. It is vital to be physically healthy and psychologically prepared for the climb.

b) Duration: The walk to Rainbow Mountain normally takes a whole day, beginning early in the morning and returning in the afternoon.

c) Trekking Routes: There are various trekking routes to Rainbow Mountain, with the most common starting point being Quesiuno. Alternatively, some trips give the option of horseback riding part of the route for those preferring a less difficult experience.

d) Scenic Views: The walk provides stunning views of the surrounding Andean terrain, including snow-capped peaks, glacial lakes, and herds of llamas and alpacas grazing in the highlands.

e) Rest places: There are rest places throughout the way where you may regain your breath, take in the landscape, and engage with local Quechua-speaking people.

4. Altitude Sickness:

a) Symptoms: Altitude sickness, commonly known as acute mountain sickness (AMS), may afflict persons at high elevations. Symptoms include headaches, nausea, dizziness, and shortness of breath.

b) Prevention: To decrease the danger of altitude sickness, acclimatize in Cusco for at least two to three days before starting the journey. Stay hydrated, avoid alcohol, and take it easy during the opening days at high altitude.

c) Treatment: If you suffer symptoms of altitude sickness, descend to a lower altitude immediately and seek medical assistance if the symptoms continue or worsen.

5. Cultural Experience:

a) Local Quechua villages: During the journey, you will visit local Quechua-speaking villages that have kept their old rituals and way of life.

b) Cultural Etiquette: Show respect for local traditions and customs by obtaining permission before taking images of individuals and their items. Learn a few simple Quechua words to converse with the people and exchange smiles and pleasantries.

c) Offerings: Some local communities may give blessings or Pachamama (Mother Earth) rites to visitors as a means of greeting them and requesting protection on their trip.

6. Essential Packing List:

a) Layered Clothing: Pack warm and breathable layers, since the weather may change fast in the Andes.

b) robust Footwear: Wear comfortable and robust hiking footwear with ankle support for the tough terrain.

c) Sun Protection: Don't forget sunscreen, sunglasses, and a wide-brimmed hat to protect yourself from the powerful high-altitude sun.

d) Water and Snacks: Carry enough water to remain hydrated, along with energy bars and snacks for the journey.

g) Rain Gear: Pack a waterproof jacket and rain cover for your backpack to prepare for unexpected rain showers.

7. Environmental Conservation:

a) Responsible Trekking: Follow the "Leave No Trace" guidelines to minimize your influence on the environment. Carry out any rubbish and litter, and avoid upsetting animals.

b) Respect Local Regulations: Abide by the rules provided by park rangers and local authorities to guarantee the preservation of the natural environment.

Ausangate Trek

Nestled in the Andes Mountains of Peru, the Ausangate Trek is a spectacular and secluded expedition that gives an immersive trip into the heart of the Andean environment. With its towering peaks, bright glacial lakes, and interactions with indigenous Quechua-speaking villages, the Ausangate Trek has become a sought-after destination for daring travellers seeking a unique and remarkable adventure. This thorough guide includes crucial information for travellers wishing to go on the Ausangate Trek, including path alternatives, hiking difficulties, cultural interactions, preparatory suggestions, and the ideal time to visit.

1. Overview of Ausangate Trek:

a) Location: The Ausangate Trek is situated southeast of Cusco, near the Ausangate Mountain, which is the tallest peak in the Cusco area and one of the holiest mountains in Andean civilization.

b) Altitude: The journey reaches elevations of above 5,000 meters (16,400 feet), making it a tough high-altitude excursion.

c) length: The length of the walk varies depending on the selected route, ranging from

4 to 7 days. Most hikes start and conclude in the town of Tinqui.

d) **Highlights:** The Ausangate Trek provides beautiful vistas, including snow-capped peaks, glacial lakes, hot springs, and interactions with local herders and their llamas and alpacas.

2. Trail Options:

a) **Classic Ausangate Circuit:** The classic Ausangate Circuit is the most popular route, requiring roughly 5 to 7 days to complete. It is a tough but rewarding adventure that circumnavigates the Ausangate Mountain.

b) **Shortened Routes:** For those with limited time or wishing for a less arduous trip, there are shorter variants of the Ausangate Circuit that may be done in 4 to 5 days.

c) One-Day trip: For tourists with modest trekking expertise, a one-day trip from Tinqui to the Rainbow Mountain viewpoint provides a glimpse of the spectacular Andean scenery.

3. Trekking Difficulty:

a) Physical Fitness: The Ausangate Trek is considered tough owing to its high heights and harsh terrain. Trekkers should be physically fit and prepared for lengthy and steep ascents and descents.

b) Altitude Acclimatization: Spend at least two to three days acclimatizing in Cusco or other high-altitude destinations before starting the walk to decrease the risk of altitude sickness.

c) Hiking Gear: Proper trekking gear, including sturdy hiking boots, warm layers, rain gear, and a well-fitted backpack, is important for a pleasant and safe excursion.

4. Cultural Encounters:

a) Local Quechua villages: The Ausangate area is home to traditional Quechua-speaking villages that have kept their old rituals and way of life.

b) Campsite Homestays: Some treks provide the chance to stay with local families in their traditional houses, offering a real cultural experience.

b) holy Mountain: Ausangate is regarded a holy mountain in Andean culture, and residents conduct traditional rites and rituals to pay reverence to its spiritual importance.

5. Best Time to Visit:

a) Dry Season: The optimum time to hike Ausangate is during the dry season, which spans from April to October. The weather is normally clear, with solid conditions for hiking.

b) Rainy Season: The rainy season, from November to March, delivers significant rains and tough hiking conditions. Trails may become muddy and treacherous, and certain routes may be temporarily blocked owing to landslides.

c) Weather Variability: Despite the dry season, weather in the Andes may be unpredictable. Trekkers should be prepared for rapid variations in temperature and weather conditions.

6. Wildlife and Flora:

a) Andean species: The Ausangate area is home to a variety of species, including vicuñas, llamas, alpacas, and Andean condors. Patient walkers may get the opportunity to glimpse these secretive animals.

b) Unique Flora: The walk shows various flora, including resilient species that flourish in the high-altitude climate, contributing to the region's natural beauty.

7. Environmental Conservation:

a) Responsible Trekking: Practice "Leave No Trace" guidelines to minimize your influence on the environment. Carry out any rubbish and litter and respect the natural environment.

b) Use Local Services: Support local communities by employing local guides, porters, and chefs. This helps to the sustainable growth of the area.

c) Respect Local Customs: Respect the cultural history and customs of the local communities by requesting permission before taking images and conforming to local restrictions.

Manu National Park

Manu National Park, situated in the Cusco region of Peru, is a huge and biodiverse protected area that provides a unique and immersive experience for nature aficionados and daring travellers. Designated as a UNESCO World Heritage Site and a Biosphere Reserve, Manu National Park is famous for its virgin rainforests, high-altitude grasslands, and diverse fauna. This thorough book includes crucial information for travellers wanting to visit Manu National Park, including its biodiversity, ecosystems, tour choices, cultural experiences, conservation initiatives, and suggestions for responsible and sustainable tourism.

1. Overview of Manu National Park:

a) Location: Manu National Park is located in southeastern Peru, encompassing an area of roughly 1.5 million hectares (3.7 million acres).

b) Biodiversity: The park is one of the most biodiverse locations on Earth, supporting a vast variety of plant and animal species, including over 800 bird species, 200 mammal species, and hundreds of plant species.

c) Ecosystems: Manu National Park has varied ecosystems, including lowland Amazon rainforests, cloud forests, and Andean grasslands, allowing an unmatched chance to explore numerous habitats in one site.

2. Getting to Manu National Park:

a) entry Points: The primary entry points to Manu National Park are Cusco and the town of Puerto Maldonado. From either site, travellers may access the park via numerous tour companies providing guided excursions.

b) Road and River Access: The route to Manu National Park frequently entails a mix of road travel and river boat rides to access the various zones within the park.

3. Tour Options and Activities:

a) Guided Tours: The best method to visit Manu National Park is via guided tours lead by skilled local guides who are knowledgeable about the region's environment and animals.

b) Wildlife Watching: Visitors may go on wildlife-watching tours to view notable species such as jaguars, huge otters, macaws, tapirs, and capuchin monkeys.

c) Birdwatching: Birdwatching at Manu National Park is a pleasant experience, with possibilities to witness a varied variety of bird species, including the colorful Andean cock-of-the-rock and the harpy eagle.

d) Cultural Encounters: Cultural visits with local indigenous people give insights into their traditional way of life, including their understanding of medicinal herbs and sustainable agricultural techniques.

e) Canopy Walkways: Some tour companies provide canopy walkways that enable tourists to explore the rainforest canopy and see life in the trees.

4. Manu National Park's Zones:

a) Cultural Zone: The Cultural Zone is the most accessible portion of the park and provides cultural interactions with the Matsigenka and Yine indigenous people.

b) Reserved Zone: The Reserved Zone is more isolated and tightly protected, enabling tourists to explore virgin rainforests and see a diverse diversity of species.

c) Manu Biosphere Reserve: The Biosphere Reserve comprises both the Cultural Zone and the Reserved Zone, fostering conservation and sustainable development in the area.

5. Conservation Efforts:

a) Biodiversity Protection: Manu National Park is crucial for the survival of various endangered and endemic species, and conservation efforts strive to maintain these distinct habitats.

b) Sustainable tourist: Tour companies in the area adhere to sustainable tourist principles, limiting environmental effect and helping local communities.

c) Research and Education: Scientific research and educational efforts are done to better understand the park's ecosystems and create awareness about the significance of biodiversity protection.

6. Responsible Tourism:

a) Respect Wildlife: Observe wildlife from a safe distance and avoid feeding or handling animals to prevent disruption and retain their natural behavior.

b) Reduce Plastic Waste: Bring reusable water bottles and containers to reduce plastic waste and maintain a "Leave No Trace" strategy throughout your stay.

c) Support Local Communities: Choose tour operators who highlight local community engagement and contribute to sustainable development programmes.

d) Comply with Park rules: Follow all park rules and recommendations to conserve the fragile ecosystems and safeguard the species inside the park.

7. Best Time to Visit:

a) Dry Season: The optimum time to visit Manu National Park is during the dry season from May to October. The weather is often drier and more suitable for exploring.

b) Rainy Season: The rainy season from November to April brings severe rainfall and floods, which may impede access to specific regions of the park.

Chapter 11: Sustainable Travel in Cusco

As one of the most popular tourist sites in Peru, Cusco offers a rich cultural history, awe-inspiring vistas, and historical treasures. To guarantee the preservation of its natural and cultural riches for future generations, sustainable travel habits are necessary. Sustainable tourism in Cusco attempts to reduce the environmental effect, help local populations, and create a greater awareness of the region's cultural and biological value. This thorough guide contains critical information for travellers looking to practice sustainable travel in Cusco, including responsible tourism initiatives, eco-friendly hotels, ethical activities, cultural immersion, conservation efforts, and advice to reduce their ecological imprint.

1. Understanding Sustainable Travel:

a) Definition: Sustainable travel, often known as responsible or eco-friendly travel, entails making mindful decisions that help the environment, local communities, and cultural heritage.

b) concepts: Sustainable travel is governed by concepts such as lowering carbon emissions, helping local economies, honouring cultural norms, and encouraging wildlife protection.

c) Positive Impacts: By practicing sustainable travel, travellers may contribute to the well-being of places, promote local livelihoods, and safeguard natural resources.

2. Minimizing Environmental Impact:

a) Transportation: Opt for eco-friendly transportation choices, such as public buses or shared shuttles, to decrease carbon emissions.

Consider walking or cycling for shorter distances.

b) **Waste Reduction:** Avoid single-use plastics and carry a reusable water bottle and shopping bag. Properly dispose of rubbish in designated recycling containers.

c) **Energy Conservation:** Conserve energy by turning off lights, air conditioning, and electrical gadgets when not in use. Choose lodgings that promote energy-efficient techniques.

d) **Water Conservation:** Practice water conservation by taking shorter showers and reusing towels wherever feasible. Be aware of water consumption during hikes and trips.

3. Supporting Local Communities:

a) Local Products: Purchase locally manufactured souvenirs and crafts to help local craftspeople and encourage the local economy.

b) Community-Based Tourism: Choose community-based tourism programmes that directly benefit local communities and engage them in decision-making processes.

c) Homestays and Cultural Experiences: Opt for homestays and cultural experiences with local families to learn about their way of life, traditions, and customs.

d) Ethical Animal Encounters: Avoid participation in activities that entail the exploitation of animals, such as captive animal attractions or riding animals for amusement.

4. Responsible Sightseeing and Activities:

a) Respect Cultural Sites: When visiting historical and cultural sites, obey established restrictions and avoid touching or removing objects.

b) Nature Exploration: Stick to established trails and routes for nature hikes and excursions to avoid damage to animals and flora.

b) Ethical Wildlife Encounters: Choose wildlife encounters that promote animal care and conservation. Observe animals from a safe distance and avoid feeding or touching them.

d) Local Guides: Hire local guides who have in-depth knowledge of the region's history, culture, and environment. They may deliver a more meaningful and real experience.

5. Eco-Friendly Accommodations:

a) Green accredited: Look for lodgings that are accredited for their eco-friendly measures, such as recycling, energy conservation, and water-saving programmes.

b) Sustainable Infrastructure: Stay in hotels that employ renewable energy sources, eco-friendly building materials, and support sustainable waste management.

c) Local Sourcing: Choose hotels and lodges that source food and supplies from local vendors to assist the area economy.

6. Conservation Efforts:

a) Support Conservation groups: Contribute to conservation efforts by supporting local and international groups striving to safeguard Cusco's biodiversity and cultural legacy.

b) Participate in Eco-initiatives: Participate in eco-volunteer programs and conservation initiatives that assist restore natural areas and safeguard endangered species.

c) Sustainable Trekking: Opt for trekking providers who follow Leave No Trace principles, reduce route erosion, and protect animal habitats.

7. Cultural Immersion:

a) Learn simple words: Learn a few simple words in Spanish or Quechua to connect with people and show respect for their language and culture.

b) Attend Local Events: Participate in traditional festivals and events to obtain insight into local customs, music, and dancing.

b) enjoy Local Cuisine: Explore local restaurants and enjoy traditional Peruvian cuisine crafted using locally sourced ingredients.

Responsible Tourism Practices

Cusco, Peru, a city rich in history, culture, and natural beauty, draws people from all across the globe. To preserve the long-term survival of this valued destination and to safeguard its natural and cultural legacy, ethical tourism practices are vital. Responsible tourism in Cusco focuses on reducing the environmental effect, helping local people, conserving cultural integrity, and fostering ethical animal interactions. This thorough guide contains critical information for travellers looking to practice responsible tourism in Cusco, including eco-friendly projects, ethical tours, cultural appreciation, conservation efforts, and recommendations for being a responsible traveler.

1. Understanding Responsible Tourism:

a) Definition: Responsible tourism, often known as sustainable or ethical tourism, entails making intentional decisions that help the environment, local communities, and cultural heritage.

b) Principles: Responsible tourism principles include limiting negative consequences, supporting local economies, respecting cultural norms, and encouraging environmental protection.

c) Positive Impact: By adopting responsible tourism practices, travellers may contribute to the well-being of Cusco, support local livelihoods, and maintain its distinctive character for future generations.

2. Minimizing Environmental Impact:

a) Eco-Friendly Transportation: Choose eco-friendly transportation choices, such as walking, cycling, or utilising public transit, to minimise carbon emissions.

b) Waste Reduction: Avoid single-use plastics and carry a reusable water bottle, shopping bag, and utensils. Properly dispose of rubbish in designated recycling containers.

c) Energy Conservation: Conserve energy by turning off lights, air conditioning, and electrical gadgets when not in use. Choose lodgings that promote energy-efficient techniques.

d) Water Conservation: Practice water conservation by taking shorter showers and reusing towels wherever feasible. Be aware of water consumption during hikes and trips.

3. Supporting Local Communities:

a) **Local Products:** Purchase locally manufactured souvenirs and crafts to help local craftspeople and encourage the local economy.

b) **Community-Based Tourism:** Opt for community-based tourism activities that directly benefit local communities and engage them in decision-making processes.

c) **Homestays and Cultural Experiences:** Engage in homestays and cultural experiences with local families to learn about their way of life, traditions, and customs.

d) **Ethical Shopping:** Support fair trade activities and avoid buying items derived from endangered or protected species.

4. Ethical Sightseeing and Activities:

a) Respect Cultural Sites: When visiting historical and cultural sites, obey established restrictions and avoid touching or removing objects.

b) Nature Exploration: Stick to established trails and routes for nature hikes and excursions to avoid damage to animals and flora.

c) Ethical Wildlife Encounters: Choose wildlife encounters that promote animal care and conservation. Observe animals from a safe distance and avoid feeding or touching them.

d) Local Guides: Hire local guides who have in-depth knowledge of the region's history, culture, and environment. They may deliver a more meaningful and real experience.

5. Eco-Friendly Accommodations:

a) Green accredited: Look for lodgings that are accredited for their eco-friendly measures, such as recycling, energy conservation, and water-saving programmes.

b) Sustainable Infrastructure: Stay in hotels that employ renewable energy sources, eco-friendly building materials, and support sustainable waste management.

b) Local Sourcing: Choose hotels and lodges that source food and supplies from local vendors to assist the area economy.

6. Conservation Efforts:

a) Support Conservation groups: Contribute to conservation efforts by supporting local and international groups striving to safeguard Cusco's biodiversity and cultural legacy.

b) Participate in Eco-initiatives: Participate in eco-volunteer programs and conservation initiatives that assist restore natural areas and safeguard endangered species.

c) Sustainable Trekking: Opt for trekking providers who follow Leave No Trace principles, reduce route erosion, and protect animal habitats.

7. Cultural Appreciation:

a) Learn simple words: Learn a few simple words in Spanish or Quechua to connect with people and show respect for their language and culture.

b) Attend Local Events: Participate in traditional festivals and events to obtain insight into local customs, music, and dancing.

b) enjoy Local Cuisine: Explore local restaurants and enjoy traditional Peruvian cuisine crafted using locally sourced ingredients.

8. Tips for Responsible Travel:

a) Be Informed: Research local customs, traditions, and cultural norms before visiting Cusco to demonstrate respect and admiration for the local way of life.

b) Dress Appropriately: Dress modestly while visiting religious places and communities, honouring their cultural norms.

c) Reduce Plastic Waste: Bring reusable water bottles and containers to avoid plastic waste and maintain a "Leave No Trace" strategy throughout your stay.

d) help Local Initiatives: Choose responsible tour operators and lodgings that stress sustainability and help local communities.

Community-Based Tourism Initiatives

Community-Based Tourism (CBT) programmes in Cusco, Peru, provide a unique and genuine travel experience that goes beyond standard tourist sites. Cusco, a city steeped in history and culture, is home to numerous indigenous populations with distinct customs and ways of life. CBT projects seek to strengthen these local communities by integrating them in the tourist business, protecting their cultural history, and giving visitors with immersive and meaningful experiences. This thorough book discusses the core of Community-Based Tourism in Cusco, its advantages, examples of successful programmes, cultural exchanges, economic effect, and suggestions for visitors to participate ethically.

1. Understanding Community-Based Tourism:

a) Definition: Community-Based tourist includes the active engagement of local communities in tourist planning, management, and benefits sharing.

b) Principles: CBT aspires to promote sustainable development, empower local communities, conserve cultural heritage, and increase tourists' awareness of local traditions and customs.

c) Positive Impact: By participating in CBT programmes, visitors may help to the well-being of local people and develop a greater understanding for the region's cultural and ecological variety.

2. Benefits of Community-Based Tourism:

a) Empowerment: CBT projects benefit local communities by giving chances for economic diversification and exhibiting their culture to a larger audience.

b) Cultural Preservation: CBT helps conserve indigenous customs, dialects, and artisanal activities that may otherwise be at danger of dying away.

c) Enhanced Travel Experiences: CBT gives tourists real and immersive experiences, promoting genuine relationships with local people and their way of life.

d) Environmental Conservation: CBT projects frequently focus eco-friendly activities, encouraging responsible tourism and safeguarding natural resources.

3. Successful Community-Based Tourism Initiatives in Cusco:

a) Amaru village: The Amaru village provides tourists hands-on experiences in traditional weaving and agricultural activities, enabling travelers to learn about Andean culture from local specialists.

b) Huilloc Community: Huilloc provides homestay experiences, providing travellers the ability to live with a local family and join in their everyday activities, such as farming and weaving.

c) Misminay Community: Misminay presents traditional dances, music, and food during cultural events, offering guests with a real Andean experience.

d) Chinchero Community: The Chinchero community shows its textile-making heritage via workshops, enabling visitors to participate and support local craftsmen.

4. Cultural Interactions in Community-Based Tourism:

a) Language and Communication: Learning simple phrases in Spanish or Quechua may substantially increase cultural relations and demonstrate respect for the native language.

b) Respectful Observance: Observe and respect local customs and traditions, obtaining permission before taking pictures and participating in rituals.

c) Active Participation: Engage in community activities, such as traditional dancing or weaving, under the leadership of local experts.

d) Cultural Immersion: Homestay experiences give unique possibilities to engage in the local culture and way of life.

5. Economic Impact of Community-Based Tourism:

a) Community Empowerment: CBT projects produce money and develop job possibilities for community people, decreasing economic dependency on agriculture or resource exploitation.

b) Revenue Distribution: The cash earned through CBT is generally reinvested in community development initiatives, such as schools, health facilities, or infrastructure upgrades.

b) **Cultural Pride:** By presenting their traditions and practises, local communities develop a feeling of cultural pride and identity, enhancing social cohesiveness.

6. Responsible Engagement in Community-Based Tourism:

a) Choose Reputable Operators: Select tour operators who stress community participation, sustainability, and fair recompense for community people.

b) Respect Local Norms: Adhere to norms provided by the community, such as suitable dress code and conduct during rituals or visits to holy locations.

b) Minimize Environmental Impact: Follow Leave No Trace principles, prevent littering, and utilise eco-friendly transportation alternatives.

Chapter 12: Traveling with Kids in Cusco

Traveling with kids to Cusco, Peru, provides a fantastic chance for families to enjoy a rich cultural history, magnificent landscapes, and old Incan monuments. Cusco, originally the capital of the Inca Empire, is a city rich in history and offers several family-friendly activities and experiences. This comprehensive guide provides essential information for tourists traveling with kids to Cusco, including family-friendly attractions, safety considerations, kid-friendly accommodations, health tips, cultural experiences, and practical advice to ensure a memorable and enjoyable trip for the whole family.

1. Preparing for the Trip:

a) vaccines and Health Precautions: Check with your doctor or a travel health clinic about recommended vaccines and health precautions for going to Peru.

b) Altitude Acclimatization: Cusco is situated at high altitude, therefore youngsters can be more prone to altitude sickness. Plan for slow acclimatization and allow for relaxation upon arrival.

c) Packing Essentials: Pack required prescriptions, a first-aid kit, comfortable clothes, and proper footwear for touring the city and nearby regions.

d) Family Travel Insurance: Ensure you have adequate travel insurance that covers medical emergencies, trip cancellations, and lost possessions.

2. Family-Friendly Attractions in Cusco:

a) Sacsayhuaman: Kids will appreciate exploring the towering stone walls and climbing the vast terraces at this historic Incan citadel.

b) San Blas District: The lovely streets of San Blas are great for leisurely family strolls, with local art galleries, handicraft stores, and bright murals.

c) Plaza de Armas: The main plaza of Cusco provides a bustling environment, where families can enjoy local street performers and explore the city's colourful culture.

d) Planetarium Cusco: A visit to the planetarium gives a fantastic chance for youngsters to learn about Incan astronomy and stargaze.

f) ChocoMuseo: Kids may join in chocolate-making classes, learn about the cocoa bean-to-bar process, and enjoy sampling delectable delicacies.

f) **Cusco Children's Museum (Museo de Arte Precolombino):** This interactive museum shows Pre-Columbian art and provides fascinating exhibits appropriate for youngsters.

3. Family-Friendly Excursions:

a) **Sacred Valley Tour:** Take a family-friendly tour of the Sacred Valley, seeing Pisac Market, Ollantaytambo, and other Incan sites along the route.

b) **Machu Picchu:** A family excursion to Machu Picchu is an amazing experience. Consider using the rail or a family-friendly trekking path to reach the citadel.

c) **Rainbow Mountain:** Older youngsters may enjoy a day excursion to Rainbow Mountain, a spectacular natural marvel famed for its bright hues.

d) Pisaq Ruins climb: Families may take a modest climb to the Pisaq Ruins, where they can explore the historic terraces and enjoy lovely valley views.

4. Kid-Friendly Accommodations:

a) Family Suites: Look for places with family suites or connected rooms to ensure everyone has a pleasant visit.

b) Child-Friendly features: Choose hotels with features such as play areas, pools, and family-friendly eating choices.

b) Location: Opt for strategically placed lodgings to have easy access to sights and eateries.

d) Check Reviews: Read reviews from other families to verify the hotel suits your family's requirements.

5. Safety Considerations:

a) Altitude: Be wary of altitude sickness, and take it easy during the first several days of your vacation to acclimatise.

b) Hydration: Keep youngsters well-hydrated, particularly at higher altitudes, to avoid dehydration.

c) Sanitation: Stick to bottled or boiled water and practice proper hand hygiene to avoid gastrointestinal troubles.

d) Food Choices: Choose reputed restaurants and cafes, and avoid raw or undercooked food.

e) Sun Protection: Apply sunscreen, wear hats, and clothe youngsters in light, protective clothing to shelter them from the sun.

6. Cultural Experiences:

a) Traditional Music and Dance: Attend local cultural events to expose youngsters to traditional Andean music and dance.

b) Local Crafts: Engage youngsters in shopping for traditional crafts at local markets and educate them about the rich cultural value of these products.

c) Quechua Language: Learn simple phrases in Quechua, the indigenous language of the Andes, to engage with people and demonstrate admiration for their culture.

d) Traditional Food: Encourage youngsters to eat native Peruvian meals, such as ceviche and lomo saltado, to experience the tastes of the area.

7. Practical Advice for Traveling with Kids:

a) Time Management: Plan your activities to meet youngsters' energy levels and provide for rest intervals when required.

b) Bring Snacks: Pack healthy snacks for the youngsters to keep them energetic throughout excursions.

c) Plan Ahead: Pre-book excursions and activities to reserve your position and prevent disappointment.

d) Family connection: Engage in activities that enhance family connection, such as sharing trip experiences and making memories together.

Family-Friendly Activities

Cusco, Peru, is a mesmerising location that provides a multitude of family-friendly activities for guests of all ages. As the historic capital of the Inca Empire, Cusco is rich in history, culture, and natural beauty, making it a great site for a family holiday. This thorough guide examines a variety of family-friendly activities in Cusco, including visits to historical landmarks, cultural experiences, outdoor excursions, animal encounters, and interactive learning opportunities. With something for every member of the family, Cusco promises to create enduring memories and amazing experiences.

1. Exploring Incan Ruins:

a) **Sacsayhuaman:** A visit to the spectacular Sacsayhuaman, an old Incan citadel, allows youngsters an opportunity to marvel at the towering stone walls and enjoy panoramic views of Cusco.

b) **Ollantaytambo:** Kids may visit the well-preserved Ollantaytambo ruins, ascending the terraces and imagine what life was like in an Incan fortress.

c) **Pisaq Ruins:** Take a family-friendly trip to the Pisaq ruins, where youngsters may uncover old terraces and meet llamas and alpacas along the route.

d) **Moray Agricultural Terraces:** Explore the amazing Moray agricultural terraces, which resemble an amphitheater, and learn about Incan farming practises.

2. Cultural Experiences:

a) ChocoMuseo: A visit to the ChocoMuseo gives a pleasant experience for youngsters to learn about the cocoa bean-to-bar process and make their own chocolate delicacies.

b) Cusco Children's Museum (Museo de Arte Precolombino): The museum includes interactive displays and hands-on activities, giving an interesting introduction to Pre-Columbian art and culture.

c) Planetarium Cusco: Kids can learn about Incan astronomy, stargaze, and engage in interactive presentations at the Planetarium Cusco.

d) Local Markets: Take youngsters to the colorful local markets, such as San Pedro Market, to enjoy the lively environment and try local delicacies and fruits.

3. Outdoor Adventures:

a) Horseback Riding: Enjoy horseback riding trips in the neighbouring region, affording breathtaking views of the Andean environment.

b) Zipline Adventure: For adventurous families, ziplining in the Sacred Valley delivers an amazing adventure among gorgeous natural environment.

b) Family-Friendly walks: Choose from different family-friendly walks, such as the short hike to the Temple of the Moon or the Maras salt ponds.

d) Rafting on the Urubamba River: Older kids may enjoy the exhilaration of white-water rafting on the Urubamba River, escorted by skilled guides.

4. Machu Picchu Adventure:

a) Train Journey to Machu Picchu: Take a family-friendly train journey to Machu Picchu, providing breathtaking vistas and a pleasant ride for youngsters.

b) Kid-Friendly Trekking: For families with older kids, try the family-friendly Inca Trail or the shorter alternative hikes to Machu Picchu.

c) Guided Tours: Engage a professional guide to make the most of your visit to Machu Picchu and help youngsters grasp the importance of the historic fortress.

d) Sun Gate Hike: Hike to the Sun Gate for a beautiful vista of Machu Picchu and a feeling of achievement for the entire family.

5. Wildlife Encounters:

a) Alpaca and Llama Farms: Visit nearby farms to meet friendly alpacas and llamas, providing youngsters a chance to feed and engage with these peaceful creatures.

b) Mariposario de Machupicchu: The Butterfly House in Aguas Calientes shows a variety of beautiful butterflies, giving a wonderful educational experience.

c) Quillabamba Coffee farms: Take a family-friendly tour to learn about coffee farming and production at Quillabamba's gorgeous farms.

6. Interactive Learning:

a) Cooking Classes: Enroll in a family cooking class to learn how to create classic Peruvian cuisine and have a great dinner together.

b) Andean Music and Dance Workshops: Participate in Andean music and dance workshops, where youngsters may learn traditional songs and dance techniques.

c) Traditional Weaving Workshops: Engage in a traditional weaving session to produce crafts and learn about the importance of Andean textiles.

d) Quechua Language Lessons: Learn simple phrases in Quechua, the indigenous language of the Andes, to engage with people and demonstrate admiration for their culture.

7. Safety Considerations:

a) Altitude Sickness: Be careful of altitude sickness and take it easy upon arriving in Cusco to allow for acclimatization, particularly for youngsters.

b) Food and Water Safety: Stick to bottled or boiled water and dine at reputed restaurants to avoid gastrointestinal troubles.

b) Sun Protection: Apply sunscreen, wear hats, and clothe youngsters in light, protective clothing to shelter them from the sun.

8. Practical Tips:

a) Time Management: Plan activities to meet youngsters' energy levels and provide for rest intervals when required.

b) Pack Snacks: Bring healthy snacks to keep youngsters energetic throughout trips.

c) Engage with Locals: Encourage youngsters to engage with local children and learn about their culture and way of life.

Tips for Parents

Traveling to Cusco, Peru, with children may be an exciting and rewarding experience for the entire family. As the ancient capital of the Inca Empire, Cusco provides a plethora of historical, cultural, and natural attractions that will capture children's imaginations. However, traveling with kids in a foreign place involves some preparation and smart planning to guarantee a safe and happy journey. This thorough book gives critical suggestions for parents coming to Cusco with children, including health precautions, safety concerns, family-friendly activities, cultural experiences, transportation, and practical guidance to create lasting memories and meaningful experiences for everyone.

1. Health Precautions:

a) immunisations: Consult with your doctor or a travel health centre to confirm that all essential immunisations for travel to Peru are up-to-date for both adults and children.

b) Altitude Acclimatization: Cusco is situated at high altitude, therefore youngsters can be more prone to altitude sickness. Plan for slow acclimatization and allow for relaxation upon arrival.

b) drugs: Bring a well-stocked first-aid kit with important drugs for common conditions including fever, diarrhea, and pain treatment.

d) Hydration: Keep children well-hydrated, particularly at higher altitudes, to avoid dehydration.

2. Safety Considerations:

a) Altitude Sickness: Monitor children for indications of altitude sickness, such as dizziness or headaches, and seek medical assistance if symptoms increase.

b) Food and Water Safety: Stick to bottled or boiled water and dine at reputed restaurants to avoid gastrointestinal troubles.

b) Sun Protection: Apply sunscreen, wear hats, and clothe youngsters in light, protective clothing to shelter them from the sun.

d) Personal Safety: Keep a watchful check on youngsters in busy settings, and designate a meeting spot in case of separation.

3. Family-Friendly Activities:

a) touring Incan sites: Engage youngsters with tales and traditions of the Inca Empire while touring ancient sites like Sacsayhuaman and Machu Picchu.

b) Cultural Experiences: Visit museums, marketplaces, and engage in interactive activities to teach youngsters to Peruvian culture and history.

c) Outdoor Adventures: Choose family-friendly hiking, horseback riding, and other outdoor activities that enable youngsters to appreciate Cusco's natural beauty.

d) Wildlife Encounters: Take youngsters to farms where they may meet alpacas and llamas, or visit the Butterfly House in Aguas Calientes for an up-close experience with butterflies.

4. Cultural Immersion:

a) Quechua Language: Learn simple phrases in Quechua, the indigenous language of the Andes, to engage with people and demonstrate admiration for their culture.

b) Local Customs: Teach children about local customs and traditions, and urge them to engage appropriately with locals.

b) Traditional Food: Encourage youngsters to taste native Peruvian foods to experience the flavors of the area.

5. Kid-Friendly Accommodations:

a) Family Suites: Look for places with family suites or connected rooms to ensure everyone has a pleasant visit.

b) Child-Friendly features: Choose hotels with features such as play areas, pools, and family-friendly eating choices.

b) Location: Opt for strategically placed lodgings to have easy access to sights and eateries.

d) Check Reviews: Read reviews from other families to verify the hotel suits your family's requirements.

6. Transportation:

a) kid Safety Seats: If utilising public transportation or private transfers, verify that kid safety seats are available and correctly fitted.

b) Walking and Cabs: Be careful while crossing streets with children and utilise approved taxis for safe transportation.

c) Public Buses: Choose trustworthy tour operators for day trips and excursions, and verify buses have sufficient safety precautions.

7. Practical Advice for Parents:

a) Plan Ahead: Pre-book excursions and activities to reserve your position and prevent disappointment.

b) Time Management: Plan activities to meet children's energy levels and provide for rest intervals when required.

b) Pack Smart: Bring a stroller or carrier for small children, along with food and entertainment for lengthy travels.

d) Cultural Sensitivity: Teach youngsters to respect local customs, traditions, and holy locations.

e) Family connection: Engage in activities that enhance family connection, such as sharing trip experiences and making memories together.

Chapter 13: Useful Phrases and Vocabulary

Cusco, Peru, is a city rich in history, culture, and natural beauty, making it a favourite destination for travellers from across the globe. While many residents in tourist locations may speak some English, learning a few basic words and terminology in Spanish and Quechua, the indigenous language of the Andes, may enrich your trip experience and promote meaningful contact with the local population. This thorough book contains necessary words and terminology for travellers visiting Cusco, including greetings, basic expressions, eating phrases, transit terms, and cultural etiquettes, to guarantee a more pleasurable and immersive journey.

1. Basic Greetings and Expressions:

a) Hello/Hi: Hola

c) Good morning: Buenos días

c) Good afternoon: Buenas tardes

c) Good evening: Buenas noches

e) How are you?: ¿Cómo estás? (informal) / ¿Cómo está? (formal)

f) I'm OK, thank you: Estoy bien, gracias

g) What is your name?: ¿Cuál is tu nombre? (informal) / ¿Cuál es su nombre? (formal)

h) My name is...: Mi nombre es...

i) Please: Por favor

j) Thank you: Gracias

k) You're welcome: De nada

2. Basic Conversation:

a) Excuse me: Perdón / Disculpe (formal)

b) Yes: Sí c) No: No

c) Maybe: Tal vez / Quizás

f) I don't understand: No entiendo

f) Can you assist me?: ¿Puedes ayudarme? (informal) / ¿Puede ayudarme? (formal)

g) I'm sorry: Lo siento

h) I don't speak Spanish: No hablo español

i) Do you speak English?: ¿Hablas inglés? (informal) / ¿Habla inglés? (formal)

3. Numbers and Basic Math:

a) One: Uno

b) Two: Dos

c) Three: Tres

d) Four: Cuatro

e) Five: Cinco

f) Six: Seis

g) Seven: Siete

h) Eight: Ocho

i) Nine: Nueve

j) Ten: Diez

4. Dining Phrases:

a) Menu: Menú

b) Water: Agua

c) Breakfast: Desayuno

d) Lunch: Almuerzo

e) Dinner: Cena

f) Bill/Check: Cuenta

g) I would like...: Me gustaría...

h) Can I have...?: ¿Puedo tener...?

i) Where is an excellent restaurant?: ¿Dónde hay un buen restaurante?

j) Delicious: Delicioso/a

k) Spicy: Picante

5. Transportation Terms:

a) Taxi: Taxi

b) Bus: Autobús

c) Train: Tren

d) Airport: Aeropuerto

e) Where is...?: ¿Dónde está...?

f) How much is the fare?: ¿Cuánto cuesta el pasaje?

g) Stop here, please: Pare aquí, por favor

h) Ticket: Boleto / Billete

i) Train station: Estación de tren

6. Directional Phrases:

a) Right: Derecha

b) Left: Izquierda

c) Straight: Derecho

d) Turn: Gire

e) Entrance: Entrada

f) Exit: Salida

g) Map: Mapa

h) Tourist Information: Información turística

7. Cultural Etiquette:

a) Respect for Culture: Show respect for local customs, traditions, and holy locations.

b) Greetings: Greet locals with a grin and a cheerful "Hola" or "Buenos días."

b) Politeness: Use "por favor" (please) and "gracias" (thank you) to indicate gratitude.

d) Bargaining: Bargaining is widespread in marketplaces but done politely without being unduly pushy.

d) Photography: Always seek for permission before taking images of people or their possessions.

f) Personal Space: Respect personal space and avoid touching individuals, particularly youngsters.

8. Emergency Phrases:

a) Help!: ¡Ayuda!

b) Call the police: Llame a la policía c) Call an ambulance: Llame an una ambulancia d) I need a doctor: Necesito un doctor e) I'm lost: Estoy perdido/a

f) Where is the closest hospital?: ¿Dónde está el hospital más cercano?

Chapter 14: Resources

Cusco, Peru, is a compelling place that provides a multitude of resources to enrich the trip experience of travellers. As the historic capital of the Inca Empire, Cusco is rich in history, culture, and natural beauty, drawing people from across the world. To make the most of your vacation to Cusco, it's vital to be aware of the resources accessible for travellers. This thorough guide gives specific information on resources in Cusco, including tourist information centers, transit alternatives, housing choices, culinary possibilities, currency exchange facilities, safety services, and advice for sustainable and ethical travel.

1. Tourist Information Centers:

a) iPerú: Cusco is home to multiple iPerú tourist information centers where guests may acquire maps, brochures, and professional advice on sights, excursions, and activities in the vicinity.

b) **Municipal Tourist support Office (Oficina Municipal de Asistencia al Turista):** Located in Plaza Regocijo, this office offers information and support to travellers, including counselling on safety and emergency services.

c) **Hotel Concierge:** Many hotels in Cusco have experienced concierges who can provide suggestions and assist organise sightseeing tours.

2. Transportation Options:

a) **Taxis:** Taxis are a major means of transportation in Cusco and are widely accessible throughout the city. Look for licenced taxis and agree on the fee before the journey.

b) Buses: Public buses are a cheap method to navigate throughout Cusco and its neighbouring regions. They link significant attractions and communities.

c) Private transports: For convenience and comfort, private transports may be scheduled via hotels or tour operators for airport transfers or day excursions.

d) Train to Machu Picchu: The PeruRail and Inca Rail train services offer transportation to Machu Picchu from Cusco and Ollantaytambo.

3. Accommodation Choices:

a) Hotels: Cusco provides a broad selection of hotels, from budget-friendly hostels to exquisite boutique hotels. Many hotels provide features like free Wi-Fi, breakfast, and tour booking services.

b) Guesthouses: Guesthouses create a homey ambiance and are a terrific alternative for guests wanting a more customised experience.

b) Homestays: For a true cultural experience, try staying with local families that provide homestay accommodations.

d) Airbnb: Airbnb alternatives are available in Cusco, enabling guests to rent flats or rooms in local houses.

4. Dining Opportunities:

a) Local Restaurants: Cusco features a thriving culinary scene, with various restaurants providing traditional Peruvian cuisine and foreign delicacies.

b) Street cuisine: Try local street cuisine, such as anticuchos (grilled meat skewers) and empanadas, for a sample of Peruvian delicacies.

c) Cafes and Bakeries: Enjoy a cup of freshly made Peruvian coffee or taste wonderful pastries at the various cafes and bakeries throughout the city.

d) Local Markets: Visit San Pedro Market and other local markets to experience fresh vegetables, fruits, and refreshments.

5. Currency Exchange Facilities:

a) Banks: Banks in Cusco provide currency exchange services, however it's better to exchange money at bigger branches or reputed exchange businesses.

b) ATMs: ATMs are readily accessible in Cusco, and many accept foreign cards. Be aware with transaction fees and daily withdrawal limitations.

c) Currency Exchange Kiosks: Currency exchange kiosks may be located around the city, particularly in tourist regions.

6. Safety Resources:

a) Emergency Numbers: The emergency number in Peru is 105 for the police and 116 for medical situations.

b) Travel Insurance: Ensure you have adequate travel insurance that covers medical emergencies, trip cancellations, and lost possessions.

b) Safe locations: Stick to well-lit and populated locations, particularly at night, and avoid flaunting costly things or huge sums of cash.

d) frauds: Be careful against typical travel frauds, such as overcharging, false tickets, and diversion methods.

7. Sustainable and Responsible Travel:

a) Responsible Tour companies: Choose tour companies who stress sustainability, environmental preservation, and assistance for local communities.

b) Eco-Friendly Practices: Practice eco-friendly behaviours, such as utilising reusable water bottles and bags, to decrease plastic waste.

b) Cultural Respect: Show respect for local norms and traditions, particularly while visiting holy places and partaking in cultural events.

d) Responsible Souvenir Shopping: Support local craftsmen and purchase original items, avoiding anything created from endangered animals or illicit materials.

f) Community-Based Tourism: Consider participating in community-based tourism activities that empower local communities and protect cultural heritage.

Recommended Reading

Cusco, Peru, is a city with a rich history, dynamic culture, and breathtaking surroundings, making it an excellent destination for interested tourists. To dive further into the spirit of Cusco and its surrounds, reading novels relating to the area may give significant insights, historical background, and cultural knowledge. This comprehensive guide offers a list of recommended reading for tourists visiting Cusco, including books on Inca history, Peruvian literature, travel guides, archaeological studies, and personal narratives, to enrich the travel experience and enhance the appreciation of this captivating destination.

1. Inca History and Archaeology:

a) "Lost City of the Incas" by Hiram Bingham: This classic book chronicles Hiram Bingham's study of Machu Picchu and the discovery of this mysterious Inca fortress. It gives a fascinating overview of the expedition and the importance of Machu Picchu in Inca history.

b) "The Conquest of the Incas" by John Hemming: For a thorough knowledge of the Spanish conquest of the Inca Empire, this book dives into the political, cultural, and military elements of the interaction between the Incas and the conquistadors.

c) "The Incas: People of the Sun" by Carmen Bernard: This book gives a riveting introduction to the Inca civilisation, including their beliefs, traditions, architecture, and the legacy they left behind in Cusco and beyond.

d) "The White Rock: An Exploration of the Inca Heartland" by Hugh Thomson: A modern-day investigation of the Inca heartland, this book takes readers on an adventure trip across the Andes, exploring the secrets of the ancient civilisation.

2. Peruvian Literature and Fiction:

a) "Death in the Andes" by Mario Vargas Llosa: This book by the Nobel laureate Mario Vargas Llosa crafts a narrative of mystery and suspense set in the Andean highlands, addressing themes of culture, identity, and political instability.

b) "The Bridge of San Luis Rey" by Thornton Wilder: This Pulitzer Prize-winning book narrates the tale of the collapse of a bridge in Peru and its influence on the lives of its victims, revealing insights into Peruvian culture and spirituality.

c) "The Feast of the Goat" by Mario Vargas Llosa: Another masterpiece by Vargas Llosa, this historical fiction describes the events leading to the execution of Dominican dictator Rafael Trujillo, with similarities to Latin American political history.

3. Travel Guides and Adventure Narratives:

a) "Lonely Planet Peru" by Carolyn McCarthy: A thorough travel book, "Lonely Planet Peru," gives practical information on sights, lodgings, food alternatives, and transportation for tourists visiting Cusco and beyond.

b) "Turn Right at Machu Picchu: Rediscovering the Lost City One Step at a Time" by Mark Adams: Follow the footsteps of the author as he retraces the trail of Hiram Bingham's journey to Machu Picchu, delivering a mix of history, adventure, and personal experiences.

c) "The Motorcycle Diaries" by Ernesto Che Guevara: Although not solely centred on Cusco, this renowned book chronicles Che Guevara's transformational trip through Latin America on a motorbike, including his stay in Peru and experiences with indigenous tribes.

4. Personal Narratives and Memoirs:

a) "The Last Days of the Incas" by Kim MacQuarrie: This historical tale portrays the epic conflict between the Inca Empire and the Spanish conquistadors, presenting a fascinating account of the events leading to the destruction of the Inca empire.

b) "Turn Right at Machu Picchu: Rediscovering the Lost City One Step at a Time" by Mark Adams: Follow the footsteps of the author as he retraces the trail of Hiram Bingham's journey to Machu Picchu, delivering a mix of history, adventure, and personal experiences.

c) "The Peru Reader: History, Culture, Politics" edited by Orin Starn, Carlos Iván Degregori, and Robin Kirk: This anthology provides a combination of articles, historical records, and literary pieces that dive into the complexity of Peruvian culture, history, and politics.

5. Indigenous Perspectives:

a) "The Weaving of a Dream: A Chinese Folktale" by Marilee Heyer: This wonderfully drawn children's book depicts the narrative of a little Chinese girl called Ming Li, emphasising the significance of aspirations, persistence, and cultural customs.

b) "The Book of Secrets" by Deepak Chopra: Although not directly relevant to Peru, this book examines ancient knowledge and spiritual concepts that resonate with indigenous viewpoints, establishing a deeper connection to local cultures.

6. Peruvian Cooking & Cuisine:

a) "The Art of Peruvian Cuisine" by Tony Custer: Explore the rich and scrumptious Peruvian cuisine with this cookbook, offering traditional recipes and insights into the country's culinary legacy.

b) "Ceviche: Peruvian Kitchen" by Martin Morales: This cookbook honours Peru's national dish, ceviche, and features a range of ceviche recipes and other Peruvian delights.

Helpful Websites and Apps

Cusco, Peru, is a mesmerising place that provides a plethora of historical, cultural, and natural attractions for travellers to experience. To make the most of their vacation and guarantee a seamless travel experience, tourists may take use of several websites and applications intended to give vital information, assist navigation, provide language help, and boost overall travel preparation. This thorough directory includes a selection of essential websites and applications for travellers in

Cusco, including travel guides, transportation services, language resources, lodging booking platforms, safety tools, currency converters, and cultural experiences, to make a smooth and pleasurable trip.

1. Travel Guides and Information:

a) iPerú (Website and App): The official tourist information platform of Peru, iPerú gives extensive information on Cusco's sights, activities, and cultural events. It also gives helpful recommendations, safety warnings, and contact data for tourist assistance.

b) Lonely Planet (Website and App): The famous travel guide publisher, Lonely Planet, provides thorough travel recommendations for Cusco, containing attractions, eating choices, lodgings, and critical travel information.

c) TripAdvisor (Website and App): A prominent travel review website, TripAdvisor, offers user-generated evaluations and suggestions for hotels, restaurants, and activities in Cusco, helping tourists make educated selections.

d) Google Maps (programme): Google Maps is a dependable navigation programme that gives real-time directions, transportation information, and sites of interest in Cusco. It operates offline, making it great for exploring the city on foot or via public transit.

2. Transportation Services:

a) Uber (App): Uber operates in Cusco, delivering quick and dependable trips for visitors. It gives predicted fares and permits cashless payments.

b) Cabify (service): Similar to Uber, Cabify is another ride-hailing service accessible in Cusco, offering secure and convenient transportation alternatives.

c) PeruRail (Website and App): For passengers travelling to Machu Picchu, PeruRail provides rail services from Cusco to Aguas Calientes, the entryway to the historic fortress.

d) Inca Rail (Website and App): Inca Rail is another rail service that brings visitors from Cusco to Aguas Calientes, providing several classes and facilities.

3. Language Resources:

a) Duolingo (Website and software): Duolingo is a language study software that provides Spanish courses for English speakers, enabling travellers acquire basic phrases and terminology for conversation in Cusco.

b) Google Translate (App): Google Translate is a wonderful tool for quick translation of text or voice between English and Spanish, improving connection with locals.

c) Quechua Language applications: Some applications like "Quechua by Living Tongues Institute" give materials to study Quechua, the indigenous language of the Andes.

4. Accommodation Booking Platforms:

a) Booking.com (Website and App): Booking.com provides a large choice of lodgings in Cusco, including hotels, guesthouses, and hostels, with user ratings and simple booking options.

b) Airbnb (Website and App): Airbnb offers unique housing alternatives, such as flats and homestays, providing travellers the chance to immerse themselves in local culture.

c) Expedia (Website and App): Expedia provides a range of hotels and airline packages, enabling travellers to book their lodgings and transportation together.

5. Safety Tools:

a) SafeAround (Website): SafeAround gives safety ratings for several places, including Cusco, delivering information into local safety circumstances and possible threats for travellers.

b) AlertCops (App): While initially created for Spain, AlertCops may be beneficial in Cusco for emergency circumstances, enabling users to report occurrences immediately to the police.

c) Smart Traveler (Website): The U.S. Department of State's Smart Traveler website includes travel warnings and safety information for American travellers in Peru, including Cusco.

6. Currency Converters:

a) XE Currency (Website and App): XE Currency is a reputable currency converter that gives real-time exchange rates and enables users to compute currency conversions.

b) OANDA Currency Converter (Website): OANDA Currency Converter is another handy tool for converting currencies, giving historical exchange rate data as well.

7. Cultural Experiences and Activities:

a) Withlocals (Website and App): Withlocals links guests with local hosts in Cusco, delivering unique cultural experiences, culinary excursions, and tailored activities.

b) GetYourGuide (Website and App): GetYourGuide provides a broad choice of excursions and activities in Cusco, from historical walking tours to adventurous experiences like ziplining and rafting.

c) Kichwa Tembo (Website): Kichwa Tembo provides immersive cultural encounters with indigenous tribes, supporting sustainable and ethical tourism.

Maps and Navigation

Cusco, Peru, is a city with a rich history, gorgeous architecture, and lively culture, making it a favourite destination for travellers from across the globe. Exploring Cusco's small alleyways, old ruins, and lively marketplaces may be a pleasant experience, but it also demands skilled navigation to guarantee a comfortable and flawless vacation. This thorough guide contains critical information regarding maps and navigation alternatives for tourists in Cusco, including physical maps, internet maps, GPS applications, city orientation, public transit, and safety recommendations, to help visitors make the most of their stay in this wonderful city.

1. Physical Maps:

a) Tourist Information Centers: Upon arriving in Cusco, visit the iPerú tourist information centers situated at significant sites such as the Plaza de Armas and the airport. These centers give free physical maps with thorough information on the city's major attractions, restaurants, and lodgings.

b) Hotels and Hostels: Many hotels and hostels in Cusco provide complimentary city maps at their front desks, which may be handy for arranging day excursions and seeing surrounding sights.

c) Guidebooks: Popular travel guidebooks like Lonely Planet, Rick Steves, and DK Eyewitness sometimes feature fold-out maps of Cusco, offering insights into the city's layout and important sites.

d) Printed Maps: Some bookshops and gift shops in Cusco provide printed maps that appeal exclusively to visitors, containing precise city layouts and attractions.

2. Online Maps and GPS Apps:

a) Google Maps (App and Website): Google Maps is a flexible and dependable tool for travelling Cusco. also gives real-time instructions for walking, driving, and public transit, and also enables users to download offline maps for use without an internet connection.

b) Maps.Me (App): Maps.Me is a popular offline map app that gives comprehensive maps of Cusco and other cities worldwide. It's a fantastic resource for navigating without using mobile data.

b) Waze (programme): Waze is a community-driven navigation programme that gives real-time traffic updates and alternate routes, making it ideal for driving around Cusco.

d) HERE WeGo (software): HERE WeGo is another offline map software that enables users to download maps in advance and use them without an internet connection, making it perfect for exploring Cusco on foot.

3. City Orientation:

a) **Plaza de Armas:** The Plaza de Armas is Cusco's primary plaza and acts as a reference point for orienting. Many of the city's major attractions, restaurants, and lodgings are within walking distance from the plaza.

b) **Cathedrals and Churches:** Cusco is littered with old cathedrals and churches, such as the Cusco Cathedral and the Church of the Society of Jesus (La Compañía de Jesús). These landmarks might help travellers orient themselves throughout the city.

b) **Inca Walls:** The famed Inca walls located throughout Cusco can function as navigation markers, directing travellers through the city's twisting streets and lanes.

d) City plan: Cusco's historic core boasts a grid-like plan with four major streets: Avenida El Sol, Avenida Tullumayo, Avenida del Sol, and Avenida Sol Saphi. Understanding this fundamental plan might aid travellers in navigating the city.

4. Public Transportation:

a) Public Buses: Cusco has a network of public buses that service different districts and attractions. Look for buses with proper signage or ask locals for aid in locating the relevant routes.

b) Taxi Services: Taxis are commonly accessible in Cusco and may be hailed from the street or booked via ride-hailing applications like Uber and Cabify. Always confirm that the taxi is registered and utilises a meter or agrees on a fee before commencing the route.

c) **Colectivos:** Colectivos are shared vans or minivans that run on designated routes and are a cost-effective method to travel between Cusco and other cities or attractions.

5. Safety Tips for Navigation:

a) **Carry a Map:** Always carry a paper map or have an offline map app on your smartphone to prevent getting lost in locations with poor internet availability.

b) **Be Mindful of height:** Cusco is located at a high height, which might impact navigation and orientation. Take it slowly, particularly while going uphill, and give time for acclimatization.

c) keep to Well-Lit places: When touring the city at night, keep to well-lit and crowded places, particularly in new regions.

d) Use Official travelling: Stick to official taxi services and ride-hailing apps to guarantee safe travelling throughout the city.

e) Ask for Directions: Don't hesitate to ask locals for directions if you're unclear about a specific site or landmark.

Chapter 15: Conclusion

Cusco, Peru, is a city that leaves an unforgettable impact on the hearts of its visitors. With its unique history, awe-inspiring architecture, lively culture, and magnificent surroundings, Cusco provides a genuinely remarkable travel experience. As we complete our thorough guide for visitors visiting Cusco, it is apparent that this wonderful city has much to offer to every sort of traveler, from history buffs to adventure seekers and cultural explorers. Let us summarize the essential lessons from this tour and reflect on the spirit of Cusco as a compelling vacation destination.

1. Rich Historical Heritage:

Cusco's historical importance as the ancient capital of the Inca Empire is visible in every area of the city. From the majestic Inca walls that surround its streets to the ancient remains of Sacsayhuaman and the magical citadel of Machu Picchu, Cusco is a living witness to the magnificence of the Inca civilisation. Tourists visiting Cusco have the chance to immerse themselves in the history of the Incas, marvel at their architectural genius, and learn about their cultural traditions that continue to persist to this day.

2. Vibrant Cultural Identity:

Cusco's cultural fabric is created from a diverse combination of indigenous Quechua traditions and Spanish colonial influences. The city's vivid festivals, colorful marketplaces, and energetic folkloric performances highlight the continuing vitality of its people. Tourists may participate in real cultural experiences, sample the delicacies of Peruvian cuisine, and see the genuine warmth and kindness of the natives, making Cusco a location that makes a lasting imprint on the hearts of its visitors.

3. Natural Beauty and Adventure:

Beyond its historical and cultural richness, Cusco is surrounded by breathtaking natural settings that lure daring hearts. From the gorgeous Sacred Valley with its terraced farms to the snow-capped summits of the Andes and the lush Amazon rainforest, Cusco offers a broad selection of outdoor sports and eco-adventures. Whether it's climbing the Inca Trail to Machu Picchu, rafting on the Urubamba River, or discovering the various flora and fauna in Manu National Park, nature enthusiasts will find their piece of heaven in Cusco.

4. A City of Contrasts:

Cusco is a city that embraces opposites, where old traditions coexist with modern facilities, and historic beauty meets contemporary art and food. The ancient and the modern combine perfectly, producing an appealing environment that grabs the hearts of travellers. The cobblestone lanes of the old center, dotted with colonial buildings and lively cafés, contrast with the busy markets and colourful street life. This unusual combination of old and contemporary makes Cusco an attractive destination that appeals to a broad spectrum of people.

5. Responsible and Sustainable Travel:

As tourism in Cusco continues to develop, ethical and sustainable travel practices are becoming more vital. Tourists may contribute positively to the preservation of Cusco's cultural and natural legacy by supporting community-based tourism projects, respecting local traditions, and reducing their environmental effect. By selecting ethical tour operators, staying in eco-friendly hotels, and being attentive of their travel choices, travellers help guarantee that the charm of Cusco stays intact for future generations.

6. Memorable Souvenirs:

Souvenir shopping in Cusco provides a treasure trove of unique handicrafts, fabrics, and handmade goods that represent the region's rich cultural past. From elaborately woven textiles and colorful alpaca outfits to traditional ceramics and silver jewelry, Cusco's marketplaces and artisan workshops provide an assortment of fascinating gifts to take back home as treasured keepsakes of the experience.